MOTHER KNOWS BEST

The Natural Way to Train Your Dog

MOTHER KNOWS BEST
The Natural Way to Train Your Dog

Carol Lea Benjamin

Photographs by
Stephen Lennard and Carol Benjamin

Drawings by Carol Benjamin

First Edition

HOWELL
BOOK HOUSE
New York

Macmillan General Reference
A Simon & Schuster Macmillan Company
1633 Broadway
New York, NY 10019-6785

Library of Congress Cataloging in Publication data

Benjamin, Carol Lea.
   Mother knows best.

   Includes index.
   Summary: An approach to training designed to make an obedient, reliable animal of the family dog.
   1. Dogs—Training. [1. Dogs-Training]   I. Lennard, Stephen, ill.   II. Title.
SF431.B422   1985   636.7'0887   84-27871
ISBN 0-87605-666-4

Portions of this book and some of the cartoons previously appeared in a slightly different form in the magazine *Pure-bred Dogs: American Kennel Gazette* © 1980, 1981, 1982, 1983 and *Animals* © 1983 Massachusetts Society for the Prevention of Cruelty to Animals. Some of the cartoons were previously published in *Pet Lovers' Gazette* © 1983, *Pet Lovers' Gazette*.

30 29 28 27 26 25 24 23

Printed in the United States of America

For Stephen

I don't know anything about men. I just know
what I like.

Contents

Carol Lea Benjamin

About the Author

CAROL LEA BENJAMIN is a professional dog trainer and the author of *Dog Training For Kids, Dog Tricks* (with Capt. Arthur Haggerty), *Running Basics, Dog Problems, The Wicked Stepdog* (a novel), *Cartooning For Kids* and *Nobody's Baby Now* (a novel). She writes the monthly column, Dog Trainer's Diary, for *Pure-bred Dogs: The American Kennel Gazette* and has written articles about dog behavior and other topics for *Better Homes and Gardens, Apartment Life, Medical Economics, Private Practice, The German Shepherd Dog Review, Runners World, Off Lead, Animals Magazine, Pet Lovers' Gazette* and other publications. Ms. Benjamin does seminars and clinics for dog trainers and pet owners all over the United States and has appeared on both radio and television answering questions about dog behavior and training. Ms. Benjamin lives in New York City and Gardiner, New York, with her husband, architect Stephen Lennard, and their German Shepherd Dog, Scarlet.

STEPHEN LENNARD is the Director of Planning and Project Management at Columbia University. His photographs have appeared in *Animals Magazine, Off Lead, Pet Lovers' Gazette* and *Pure-bred Dogs: The American Kennel Gazette*.

Foreword

WHEN I GRADUATED veterinary school in 1966, I had a strong background in anatomy, physiology, medicine, surgery and other ancillary subjects that I felt prepared me well to treat the medical and surgical problems of my clients' pets. Nowhere during my preveterinary curriculum nor during my four years at the N.Y.S. College of Veterinary Medicine at Cornell University was I exposed to an organized course in animal behavior or psychology.

I soon realized that many of the questions I was expected to answer and much of the advice I was expected to give were related to animal behavior. The behavior of a companion animal is probably the most important factor in determining how much an owner enjoys his or her pet. A serious problem with behavior, such as aggression, fear biting, house soiling, may lead to a pet's demise as readily as being hit by a car or developing a serious, possibly untreatable, disease condition.

Carol Benjamin's approach to understanding and directing a dog's behavior is based on the fundamental premise that the domesticated dog is recently descended from a pack animal. From his first lesson with his mother, to his interactions with his siblings and finally in his interaction with adults both inside and outside the pack, his behavior is modified and directed to establish his place in the pack. Only by understanding this system can a natural method of behavior modification and training be undertaken. Using this method we will not ask the pet to understand a new form of training. Rather, we will use the method (as closely as we can mimic it) that has been used for generations to help the individual find his or her place in a new pack/family.

JEFFREY A. LaCROIX, D.V.M.
EASTON, CONNECTICUT

Acknowledgments

The author wishes to thank the following friends, relatives and colleagues, each of whom contributed generously to the making of this book:

My agent, William Reiss; my publisher, Elsworth Howell; fellow trainers Job Evans and Marie Ehrenberg; Kathleen Harvey; Jeffrey La Croix, D.V.M.; Margaret Hoh; Bruce Wolk; Susan and Byron Bell; Rita and Bill Davis; Polly DeMille; Richard Siegel; Scott Biller; Carol and Bob Canfield; George J. Smith; Barbara Widmayer; Victoria Halboth and Stephen Lennard.

Thanks, too, to the following dogs, each of whom was kind enough to pose as "Buddy" for this book—with special thanks for those valiant few who took a correction for the purpose of educating others:

Benson, Lab mix; Deela (Christan's Starry Night), Shetland Sheepdog; Ernie (Lind-Land's Ernest Raymond), Sussex Spaniel; Franz (Ch. Charisma Grand Marnier); Standard Schnauzer; Jamie, Shepherd mix; J.J., English Springer Spaniel; Chelsea (Ch. Jacquet's Chelsea), Boxer and her puppies; Maximus, Irish

Wolfhound mix; Oliver (Oliver Fox Benjamin, CD), Golden Retriever; Fanny (Benjamin's Gold-Rush Fanny), Golden Retriever and her puppies; Polo (Sutop's Precious Puppers), Welsh Terrier and Scarlet (New Skete's Kindred Spirit), German Shepherd Dog.

The cover photo is of Am. Can. Ch. Four K's Mindy of Woodbury and her puppy, owned by John and Lynne Lounsbury (Jolly Kennels) and Ken and Bana Southworth. Photo by Stephen Lennard.

It would be unfair indeed not to thank my parents for almost always saying *yes* when my sibling and I said, "*Please* may we keep him? He followed us home." And it would be unthinkable not to thank Ollie. I miss you, Red.

© Carol Benjamin 1983

14

1
Between Man and Dog

But now ask the beasts, and they shall
teach thee

The Book of Job 12:7

EVER SINCE THE TIME when brontosaurus' humungus feet precluded any worries about crab grass and the neighborhood pterodactyl dissuaded the kids from staying out too late, the dog has been part of man's family portrait. No one is absolutely sure how he wedged himself into the picture. Perhaps it all began when he tagged along on the hunt hoping for leftovers. Later on, he may have played games with the cave children, warmed up the bed on cold nights and barked a warning when strangers approached the entrance of his cave. One way or another, perhaps with the same sure charm he wields today, the dog seems to have inspired his own domestication, attaching himself permanently to the family of man. So be it. You can't fight history.

In those simple days of yesteryear, man's skills and those of the dog were more closely matched than they are today. Each could spot the weakling in the pack who would be the most likely candidate for woolly mammoth bourguignonne. Each was a distance runner, able to travel tirelessly for hours in his bare feet. Each species was social and hunted cooperatively in groups. And each had dazzling expertise in the use of body language, as

15

So be it.

You can't fight history.

16

both eloquent speaker and able listener. Even when human language was in the grunt stage and the whole of humanity sounded like today's teen-agers, between man and dog, communication was rich. And since neither wanted to be president of IBM or win a Nobel prize, their goals were even similar—a hearty meal, a warm, dry place to sleep, a chance to reproduce and the ability to play about out of doors without getting eaten.

Way back then, when hungry carnivores were chasing our ancestors, survival was everything and it was pretty much a full-time job. Toward that end, man and dog were on the same team. Together, they figured out which way the herd had turned, found clean water, got through the night. Together, they ate, played, slept and escaped. Together, they were in or out of luck, well fed or hungry, happy or sad—and each knew how the other was feeling, though neither probably gave that fact a second thought.

No longer is the good life a hunk of meat, a warm wrap and an unoccupied cave. Things are different now. As time passed, life became more complex, subtler. Stress began pursuing us in increasingly difficult to spot guises. Along the way, we got distracted by wars, the industrial revolution, materialism, electronic gadgets. Along with such benefits as inoculations, no-iron cottons, trans-Atlantic flights and the seedless orange, there were also instant mashed potatoes, polyester, overcrowding, pollution, unemployment and nuclear wastes. Modern life has taken its toll.

Little by little, we humans began to move away from our own naturalness. We lost the ability to predict weather by looking at the early morning sky. We lost our sense of the intentions of wild animals. We lost the toughness that used to let us hunt, forage and survive in the wilderness.

Along the way, our expectations were elevated and, in the process of rising to meet them, we suffered a loss of genuine, easy communication. We lost touch with that quick understanding of basic truths we once had. Alas, we grew gullible. As our verbal language became more complicated and precise, we began to lose the ability to read significant posturing, meaningful breathing patterns, a broad range of emotional grimacing, a

> No one is absolutely sure how the dog wedged himself into the picture.

quick, pregnant glance. As our lives began to keep us apart from ourselves, each other and our dogs, we began to lose that perfect rapport we once had, so very long ago.

Gradually, a kind of generation gap developed between the species. Oh, we still loved each other. But ready, quiet, graceful, mutual education became extinct. In its place, shouting, pouting, hitting with rolled-up newspaper, isolating in the basement, garage or yard, zapping with electricity, abandonment and even euthanasia evolved. And all the while, the human race yearned for what it had lost—clean air, blue skies, a feeling of belonging to the earth and of caring for it and, for many, the sweetness of good communication that existed, once upon a time, between man and dog.

Even if we were willing to live side by side without relating as kindred spirits, we'd still need good communication in order to educate our dogs. Untutored, they can no longer fit well into our busy, complicated lives. Modern dog must walk at our sides without pulling, stay put when told, bark at the door, stay off the furniture, come when called. He must learn not to urinate on the rug, run away, eat the couch, growl over food, act as if he still lived in a cave! Time has changed our style of living and in order to keep our dogs safe and ourselves sane, we need some control. We need to teach the dog manners, commands, limits. We need to communicate efficiently again. We need help!

Help, my fellow humans, has a hairy chest and whiskers on her chin. She has already taught your puppy much—to accept leadership, to handle praise and correction with equanimity, to heed meaningful sounds, to play gently, to wait his turn, to deliver and receive affection, to copy her sterling example whenever he was able. She was a remarkable teacher, so graceful, accurate and self-contained that to watch her would take your breath away.

We can learn from her, too. We can find out how puppies learn. We can find out what works and what doesn't. We can find out how to be brief yet eloquent, effective yet kindly, civilized as well as natural. Once again, the human race can learn the secrets of natural communication by watching, understanding and copying, either in spirit or in kind, the way a mother

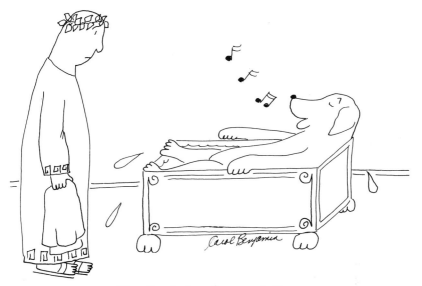

We suffered a loss of communication.

A kind of generation gap developed.

21

Once again, we can learn the secrets of natural communication.

canine raises and teaches her young. In this way, we will be assured that whatever we do to train, to praise or correct, to relate to our dogs will be effective, efficient and, beyond the shadow of a doubt, humane.

Rewards—

and punishments: Mother knows best!

24

2

Rewards and Punishments: Mother Knows Best

She was so deeply imbedded in my consciousness that for the first year of school I seem to have believed that each of my teachers was my mother in disguise.

Philip Roth
Portnoy's Complaint

WITH ALL THE assurance, serenity and natural wisdom of her species, a mother dog teaches her young with a dazzling economy of effort. She almost never has to repeat her action a second time in order to be effective. She never loses patience, gets frustrated, gives up. Yet, neither does she harm her puppies with an inappropriate use of force or an unnatural withdrawal of her affection. She knows just what to correct and precisely what to ignore. Her timing is sheer perfection. Her priorities are admirably fitting. Each mother keeps her puppies safe and, in a few short weeks, teaches them much of what they have to know in order that their survival be ensured. It is easily evident that mother knows best. She is a sterling example of teaching and loving at its finest.

A mother dog teaches her young with a dazzling economy of effort.

When you want to know the best way to reward or correct your dog for behavior you want him to repeat or eliminate, look to his mother. Her swift and fair rewards and punishments communicate clearly to the young puppies which behavior may be repeated and which should be dropped, fast. Rarely will the puppies misunderstand, willfully disobey or turn a deaf ear, so adept is she at getting her message across.

You may not want to copy the bitch exactly. Indeed, some dog owners prefer the taste of vichyssoise to dog fur and would therefore shun using "mouth on" corrections and rewards as the bitch does. But if you work in the style of the mother of your puppy, you will be assured of communicating with him. Without communication, there is no learning.

Verbal communication is well within keeping of your dog's educational heritage and his capacity to understand. The bitch uses a variety of sounds with which to communicate to the puppies. Some of the sounds relay her affection. Some call the puppies to rally around her. Some warn of danger, some of her fierce, protective anger when danger is a possibility. The puppies understand and respond.

Physical communication is very much a part of the way the mother teaches her young. Initially, her very touch is life giving, helping the whelp to begin to breathe on his own. Next her licking stimulates the digestive system of the young pup to work and triggers the elimination process. But the mother does more than clean the puppies. When they begin to see and hear and stumble about, she keeps them together, allowing only minimal exploration at first. If a puppy should stray outside the circle of safety his watchful mother prescribes, her foreleg lands on his neck and slams him to the ground. And he'll have to work at getting back in her favor, though never to the point of going long without her forgiveness.

Ancient signs, seen in packs of wild wolves, are no secret to the dog. Domesticated, tame, selectively bred to retrieve, point, herd, protect, his pack instincts still survive. The punished puppy will anxiously lick beneath his mother's chin, signaling her that he clearly understands her pack position as his superior. She, too, will speak eloquently in the old language of the wild,

27

gently biting him back across the top of his muzzle or even taking his whole head softly in her mouth. "Benevolent, but alpha," she says. She is the boss. Her puppy understands. Order is reestablished and peace reigns.

No matter how the pup transgresses, no matter how angry the bitch becomes, she never denies him his nourishment. He never goes to bed without his supper. Nor does she offer tidbits of food, treats beneath the table, extra portions of dessert to reward good behavior. Eating is eating and education is education. Mother knows best.

The primitive organism we call *dog* can neither think nor concentrate in the presence of food. His mind is aswirl with the nutty flavor of aged cheese, the potential crunchy goodness of a baked biscuit, the spicy, greasy, burning deliciousness of a small bit of salami. The odors fill his nostrils, fill his brain, hold him firm. While he seems to learn and will perform his tasks for food rewards, he is working in a robotlike fashion and not getting educated. He will repeat a pattern of behavior, in zombielike fashion, while drunk with desire for the proffered tidbit. Sadly, he will not get hooked on learning this way. His training will remain at a mediocre level with the use of rewards that are not historically valid, rewards his mother never used.

Watch a puppy, any puppy, learning at his mother's knee. He'd give her the world to hear the right tone sung from high in her throat, to be allowed to cuddle, to be petted by her smooth tongue. Moreover, his motivation to learn is built in. There's a world he's dying to explore. There are things he'd like to know. He watches everything. He experiments. He tries and tries again to meet each challenge, to learn, to expand his world, his skills, his knowledge. Like any fledgling, his curiosity triggers learning. When there are no major temptations such as food rewards to tug his mind away from the work at hand, he praises himself, he feels good to have done something new, and to have done it right.

You can see a dog learn to put two and two together. Often a green dog, on his first formal obedience lesson, will learn not merely a command; he'll also learn how to concentrate. As soon as he does, he'll begin to sneeze or just look cocky, displaying his absolute pleasure at this clearly mammoth achievement. Your added praise, "That's my good boy," reminiscent of his mother's affectionate cooing, will complete the picture.

Each subsequent experience with education will draw him. While he does have a side to his personality some might call willful, while he does want to do things his way and in his own good time, still there is that pull, the curiosity to find out what the alpha person wants, what the new word means, to test his intelligence and to feel accomplished.

A food reward is beside the point. In that, it interferes with the natural process of learning rather than aiding or augmenting it. Your verbal and physical praise, all reminders of his mother's approval, help your dog to learn—to learn for the sheer pleasure of it. This way he will work beyond the point where an artificial reward would be introduced.

Just as the puppy's mother's gentle licking or pleased throat sounds didn't stop the activity at hand from continuing, so your natural, organic and imitative praise will not stop your puppy's education from continuing. Rather than stopping the learning process to eat his treat or to seek an additional one, he will, feeling expanded and lively, work on with more energy and more motivation. The knack of great praising is to be imitative of the style and quality of the bitch. When offering approval of her young, she does not get hysterical and jump up and down. Her praise is not a break in the activity but instead an integral part of the flow. Thus, she coos to let her puppies know she's there and watching, approving and loving. You can adopt her methods in your own training program.

FIGURING OUT THE PROPER DOSAGE

There are dogs that cannot be praised at all while they are working. They get so overexcited at a touch or a word of praise that all work stops. Others need but a quiet, "Good dog," as they heel along or when you break a stay. On the other end of the spectrum, there are dogs that can take passionate manhandling and kissing for merely executing an automatic sit or a proper recall. They will work on, bursting with pride and love, but not giving you a faulty step. The type and amount of praise your dog

Benevolent—but alpha!

needs is totally individual and must be determined by observing *his* behavior, not any other dog's. He should be praised sufficiently so that he clearly gets the message, yet not enough to make him wild, silly or distracted from his tasks. Praise should not be rigidly delivered, nor harsh, nor in any way disruptive.

Corrections, on the other hand, are *supposed* to have a disruptive effect, causing the activity the dog is participating in to cease on the spot. When the bitch corrects a pup, she does so with no more harshness than is needed to get the point across. She does not prolong the correction for more time than is necessary. She is not so mild that the pup gets cheeky and continues to misbehave. She is right on target, always. You can be, too. You can find the power needed with your dog to bring him up short when he is doing something wrong, something disobedient or something that endangers his safety or your sanity. You can be as clear, swift and accurate as his mother, using either verbal corrections, physical corrections or both.

While the mother dog resorts to "teeth on" corrections, experiments and experience show that collar and leash corrections are sufficiently imitative and effective. Her slamming the puppy to the ground stops him effectively as does a good, firm, not harsh, collar and leash correction or a shake by the collar for truly errant behavior. Her verbal warnings make the puppy stop and rethink his doings. Your verbal warnings can be just as powerful.

While watching animals as they behave and function without human interference is always a very worthy part of our education about their ways, it is not necessary to stop at observation or imitation. Some of the finest innovations do come from going back to the pack or litter to see how things are done. But other exciting ideas come from going forward *while keeping that information in mind.*

When praising or correcting a puppy, the mother is limited to *here and now* behavior. What she sees is what she deals with. Humans have, using their superior intelligence, figured out some worthwhile spin-offs from observing the way dogs react in the face of *after the fact* corrections. It is worth noting that the bitch would have no need for this type of education nor the

Like mother—

like daughter. The more we know, the more we think we know, the more Mother has yet to teach us.

REWARDS

And when she was good
She was very, very good . . .

	MOTHER MIGHT	YOU MIGHT
Puppy is good		
Explores new area	Coo lovingly	"Good dog!"
Follows you	Lick puppy	Pet puppy
Plays with his toys		
Comes when called	Loving eye contact	Loving eye contact
indoors	Pant	Smile
Puppy is very good		
Responds to his name	Play with puppy	Play with puppy
Walks on leash	Take pup's head	Hug puppy
Executes a command	her mouth	
after a reminder	Make approving sounds,	"Gooood dog.
	coo	That's my
		good dog!"
Puppy is very, very good		
	Coo, lick, play,	"That's my good
Executes command on his	frolick	dog!"
own for the first time		Kiss, pet, play, act
Travels to his papers		silly, call your
without help		mother
Comes when called		
outdoors		Clap, hoot, whistle

34

PUNISHMENTS

But when she was bad she was horrid.

Henry Wadsworth Longfellow

	MOTHER MIGHT	YOU MIGHT
Puppy is bad		
Nips	Make a warning sound	"NO!"
Soils (when untrained)	Block puppy's path	Stop puppy with your hands or collar and leash, get his attention and give warning look
Begins to chew molding or chair leg (when untrained)	Give a warning look	
(other mistakes)		"Don't even think about it!"
Puppy is very bad		
Runs away when called	Growl	Give harsh verbal correction: "NO! SHAME!"
Nips repeatedly	Make harsh eye contact	
Spoiled barking	Slam puppy by placing her paw on his neck	Make harsh eye contact
(other disobedience)		Collar and leash correction
Puppy is horrid		
Growls	Grasp pup by scruff and shake	Shake pup by grasping collar and moving him back and forth a couple of times
Bites		
Eats couch		
Defacates on rug (after training)	Alpha roll, harsh eye contact, growl	Grasp pup by cheeks, his paws come up off the ground, use harsh eye contact and firm voice correction
(other major war crimes in puppies over five months old)		

Nota Bene: Mother dogs do not reward and correct their puppies for the same things we do. Mother's rewards and punishments above are for that level of activity. Ours are for that exact activity. In no case does the canine or the human hit the puppy with a rolled-up newspaper or anything else.

capacity to handle it. She cares little if the puppies destroy a stick or shred some of their bedding and "mess up the house." She is primarily concerned with their safety and can only deal with what she is seeing at the moment. If a puppy had gotten into trouble while she was gone, she'd have no way of knowing it when she returned. Nor would she be able to figure out a way to communicate her concern or displeasure. However, human educators of canines have found that *when evidence is available*, it can be used to remind a dog of a misdeed performed earlier on. The dog who has a housebreaking disaster or who tears up the couch pillows while you are out can be punished when you return by returning him to the scene of his crime, bringing him face to face with the results of his erroneous behavior and proceeding from there, like mother, as if the act had just occurred. Once reminded, then *is* now.

No one would seriously suggest that humans behave only as dogs when dealing with dogs. While it is fun indeed to get on all fours at playtime, to shove and growl and push away your nonaggressive dog in the manner in which he'd play with another dog, it is also fun and fine to communicate with your dog on *your* level, to draw him toward an understanding of human behavior and human language. However, sometimes, when there is a question as to the efficiency of a technique, to its history or to ways to make it better, it is very worthwhile to study dogs among themselves and to note the natural and organically sound process of education as it takes place dog to dog, without misunderstanding, excessive harshness, ineffectual weakness and unnecessary distractions that keep the dog's mind off his work instead of on it. There, where ancient pack laws still hold true, communication and education are still within Mother Nature's glorious and perfect design. The more we know, the more we think we know, the more Mother has yet to teach us.

3

Getting Organized

I hate women because they always know
where things are.

James Thurber
Men Against Women

No MOTHER DOG loses sleep worrying whether or not her little charges will get straight A's in obedience school, take Best in Show at Westminster or find suitable mates. Her priorities are all in the here and now, all related to survival. She supplies her puppies with a nutritious, natural diet. She tries her best to keep them clean, dry and warm. She keeps them safe from intruders—of any species. By the time she finishes one task, it's time to do the next. It's a hectic time for mothers. In seven or eight weeks, her puppies are ready to leave home. There just isn't time enough for thinking about the future—even if she was able.

Not so for us. We have both the ability and the need to think ahead. From seven or eight weeks on—and for a good, long time to come—the little puppy is in our care. We'll have him as he grows bigger, stronger, bolder, cheekier. Unlike his mom, we have concerns in addition to survival. We, too, must feed our youngster, keep him safe, warm and loved; but we also care about stains on the rug, torn-up sneakers, stolen roasts. Our priorities are more varied and more complicated than his mother's were. They are also more far reaching.

In seven or eight weeks—

her puppies are ready to leave home.

As caretakers of new puppies, we need to figure out the order of all the important things we have to teach. We even have to think about just how we'd like our puppy to behave when he's all grown up, because we don't want to do anything while he's little that will ruin things for him when he's big. In this, we are still mimicking his mother. In her brief but essential period of care of the litter, nothing she did or taught spoiled anything for the future. Quite the contrary. Busy as she was, she still taught her young some urgent manners, including respect for the alpha dog. It was this, in fact, that allows you to slip so easily into her shoes. Becoming pack leader or alpha dog makes you the pup's next natural educator and all his mother's early nurturing helped to prepare your puppy for this very event—joining a human pack and accepting a human pack leader.

Just as his mother did, we, too, must prepare our buddy (read: Buddy)* for what lies ahead. Since our demands on him will be so much more complicated than his mother's, we must weigh the importance of each thing we want to teach so that we establish priorities and don't overwhelm the little whelp by trying to do everything at once.

When you first get your little pup, you'll want to housebreak him, teach him how to walk on a leash, teach him to stay alone quietly, teach him his name. You'll want to curb any nipping, teach him not to growl or bite over food, stop destructive chewing, keep him off the furniture and discourage begging, rowdiness, jumping up. You'll want him to be loved, but not spoiled rotten; trained, but not a robot; lively, but controllable. What should you do first?

Look to his mother. Her priorities were clear because she had to deal with survival. So do you—both the puppy's and your own. Toward that end, decide what you must accomplish first. Then decide what the puppy is able to learn right away. Finally, think about what you will expect from the puppy when he's older and how you will keep those options open.

Here are some suggestions for organizing Buddy's early childhood education. Instructions for teaching all these things will be found in the following two chapters.

---

*Every dog needs a name, even a dog in a training book.

© Carol Benjamin
1981

**We, too,
must feed
our youngster.**

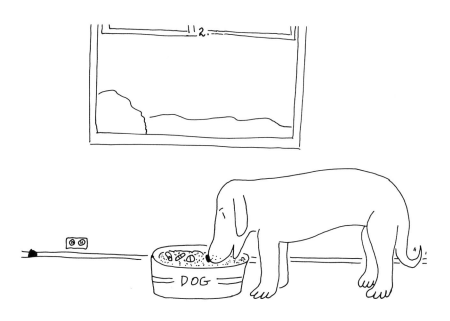

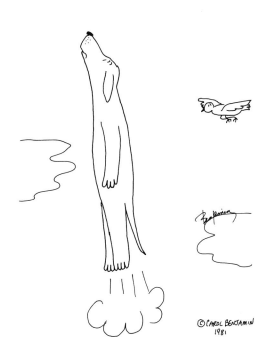

© CAROL BENJAMIN
1981

41

CURRICULUM FOR A PET PUPPY

The First Month (8-12 weeks)

Week One:

- Take puppy for veterinary check up. Stool sample is checked for worms and preventive inoculations given.

- Initiate housebreaking program.

- Teach puppy his name.

- Set up eating area, sleeping quarters (crate), toy basket.

- Begin collar and leash training.

- Watch your puppy when he plays by himself. Note his style, charm, uniqueness. Take pictures.

- Play gently and actively (not roughly) with your puppy. (Read GAMES chapter.) Have someone else take pictures.

- Tell your puppy OK whenever you feed him or hand him a toy.

- Tell your puppy OK as you walk out the door with him.

Week Two:

- As you play, gradually add simple phrases and words into the games. If the pup is retrieving, tell him TAKE IT as you throw the ball. Praise him when he brings it back to you. Tell him OUT as he drops it and praise him again.

- Continue with OK for food and going out.

- Continue with housebreaking schedule, leash training, playing and observing. This is the time to get acquainted.

Week Three:

- Begin to correct the puppy gently for nipping and for chewing on rugs, clothing, furniture. Hand him a toy to chew instead.

- Even if your puppy is not going outside, walk him around on his leash every day.

- Begin to encourage eye contact. Say WATCH ME to the pup and draw his attention to your eyes. Praise him for looking at you. This teaches the puppy to look to you for direction.

- Begin to tie pup's leash to your belt and have him trail around indoors or out wherever you go—first for a few minutes at a time, working up to an hour as it becomes easier. This will help bond the youngster to you and will help with his training.

- Begin to teach table manners, starting with NO and OK for food.

- Begin the SIT STAY, working only five minutes at a time this week.

- If you are at home most of the time, be sure that you leave the puppy alone for short periods of time during the day to get him used to your absences.

- Begin to correct the stealing of food and found objects but use prevention as your main correction.

- Begin to correct excessive barking, whining, noise making.

Week Four:

- Continue with all of the above, lengthening time pup will walk nicely on leash, beginning to cut out one of the walks in the housebreaking schedule, continuing to practice NO and OK with food once or twice a week, continuing to let the puppy explore the house while being monitored, both on and off leash.

- Add COME and DOWN STAY to your training program, now working with the puppy for ten to fifteen minutes at a time. If the puppy is going out, begin very gently to teach the HEEL.

43

- Accustom the puppy to grooming procedures—brushing, nail clipping, an occasional bath.

- Begin to play more elaborate games, naming the objects of play (BALL, BONE, FROG, etc.) and the processes as well (TAKE IT, FIND THE BALL, OUT, CATCH ME).

- Do not let the puppy run out the door. Make him wait until you say OK and praise him for exiting when you do.

By the end of the first month, your partially housebroken, partially well mannered, partially trained puppy will be on a comfortable routine. As you continue to help him with problems of etiquette, you will also continue his education as implied in his vocabulary list and as explained in future chapters. It may seem like an awful lot of work, but he's worth it. Just ask his mother!

VOCABULARY FOR A PET DOG

Many dog owners are at a loss for vocabulary when they wish to communicate with their dogs. Of course, your choice of words is not the issue. What is important is that you pace your vocabulary lessons in such a way that your dog absorbs the first few definitions before you go on to the text. And, since dogs are learning English as a second language, you must be consistent. In fact, in time, your dog, once started on the road to a better, richer vocabulary, will understand long sentences, subtle utterings, life-saving orders.

Here is a sample vocabulary for canines. With these words under his collar, any dog can live in harmony with any person, more or less. In addition, this is an appetizing peek into the future. By the time you have taught Buddy everything in this book, he will be doing all the things implied in this list—off leash and in the real world.

1. NO (Permission denied). This may be one of the first words a puppy hears, or at least that registers as a word. It is essential for every dog to know a word that stops him from urinating on the carpet, hogging the bed, running out

45

into traffic, nabbing the leg of lamb, mating beneath his station. NO is that word.

2. OK (Permission granted). Eventually, without the gift of OK, the puppy trained on NO alone could turn into a book end or lawn ornament. For the balanced, happy, obedient pet, approval is at least as important as disapproval. You can give Buddy permission to do something he'd do anyway, just to show him it's OK with you. This reenforces your position as alpha dog. It also increases the amount of positive reenforcement in your dog's life—a good thing in my book. You can use this release word to let him out of work, out of the house, into the car, at his dinner, onto your bed. Dogs learn OK instantly. They're no dummies.

3. GOOD DOG (Approval from the top). If you say GOOD DOG in the proper tone, you dog will give you the world. Saying GOOD DOG is *the* most important tool any owner has in training a dog.

4. BAD DOG (Disapproval from the top). BAD DOG, from the right lips, can be more powerful and more effective than any leash correction, any shaking, any cold shoulder, any confining, any anything you would dream of doing to your rotten, disobedient dog. He must have your approval. When you deny him that, you have already made a serious correction. Remember that when his mother corrected his errors with a stare, a growl, a clop with her foreleg, how he tried and tried to get back in her good graces. Learning to toe the mark is part of the lesson of being a dog. No puppy grows to doghood without hearing his share of BAD DOGS.

5. SIT (Plant your rump). Even an untrained dog, and I shudder at the thought, should know SIT and STAY. How else can you have any order or control? Your dog must sit while you wait at the vet, while getting his collar put on, while waiting for his bowl to be filled or the traffic light to change. Moreover, teaching him to SIT STAY will teach him how to learn, as you'll soon see.

6. STAY (Freeze). Actually, the SIT STAY is *the* way to teach vocabulary to a dog. It is through this initial

discipline, which can be done very gently and without a choke collar on a very young puppy, that the dog learns how to listen and then how to learn. What you request in the SIT STAY is clear and comprehensible *to the dog*. Therefore, in the initial teaching of the command, he can absorb the concepts of both words. He will, for example, try to move from the spot. When you return him to it, he gets the STAY part. Now he'll lie down, figuring if he's going to be stuck in the spot, he might as well get comfortable. When he is returned to the SIT position by you (gently and with patience), he learns the *exact* definition of the word SIT. By the time you finish this exercise, the dog will not be performing a feat of rump alone. Every cell in his body will be doing a SIT STAY. In this way, your dog learns two vocabulary words that stand for two separate concepts. Moreover, he learns how to learn. You will readily see the difference in the intelligent look on his face.

Furthermore, the STAY command, once added to your dog's vocabulary, not only covers a multitude of situations, but it is the beginning of teaching your dog long sentences and important concepts. It very much reenforces your alpha position. It is a great aid in keeping the dog from harm. It will come up again later in this list.

7. HEEL (Walk at my side).   HEEL is a nice thing for a dog to know, even if you live in the middle of twenty-five acres and your Buddy rarely sees a leash. First, sometime he must leave home—to see the vet, go to a dog show, go visiting, go to the boarding kennel. Second, he should leave home. He should see the world beyond your twenty-five, for his pleasure and to keep him from getting fearful of new things, of strangers, of other dogs. He needs variety in order to be well socialized. Many dogs who are raised in an ideal country setting, who are fed the best feed, who are groomed and loved and cared for, get weird when off their own property. A well-balanced animal must leave his own turf and be able to feel comfortable wherever he goes. Thus, Buddy should learn to HEEL so that you will be able to take him places neatly, easily, frequently.

8. COME (Join me).   COME needs no sales pitch as an important word in every dog's vocabulary. The aim of this book is to teach you how to teach your dog to come quickly, cheerfully and willingly when he is off leash, out of doors, even playing with *his* buddies. That's what I call a dog with a good vocabulary!

9. DOWN (Lie down).   DOWN is my all-time favorite command/vocabulary word for dogs. Executed rapidly, it can be a life saver. It can calm a dog. It can cover hours waiting anywhere with your dog. It can give you peace and quiet while you read a book, make a souffle, write a dog book. DOWN is a winner.

10. STAND (Stand).   In conformation or obedience competition, in the bathtub, under the grooming brush, to negate the automatic sit on a rainy, rainy day, STAND is a nice word to have in a dog's vocabulary.

11. GO (Move away or move away in the direction in which I am pointing or accompany me somewhere).   GO is a good word to teach dogs. Often, you can point and look forbidding and say GO and your dog will have learned it, just like that. GO, handy in its own right, becomes more interesting as the key word in sentences such as, "Do you want to go out? Go home. Go away. Go to the car. Go to your bed. Go to your crate. Go to the kitchen. Go find your ball. Go out (Leave the room)."

12. ENOUGH (Whatever you are doing was OK, but I've just changed my mind and now I want you to stop it—as opposed to NO, which means whatever you are doing is unacceptable and should never be done).   ENOUGH is taught mainly, believe it or not, by tone of voice, is usually learned rapidly and can stop excessive barking, a game of roughhousing that has gotten out of hand, any activity that is usually OK but cannot, for whatever reason, continue at this point. It can calm a dog instantly. It can give you the full attention of a dog who was, up until a moment ago, acting up or acting out. I couldn't raise a dog without it.

13. OVER and OUT.   Of course, if you fly your own plane and send radio messages to your dog, he already knows

DOWN can calm a dog.

Go to your bed!

49

OVER and OUT. In this case, however, OVER and OUT are used separately. OVER tells your dog to sail over an obstacle. You may prefer to use the word JUMP or HUP. It doesn't matter. What does matter is that jumping on command is not only useful in piling up obedience degrees; it is also good for getting white dogs over mud puddles and muddy dogs into bathtubs. You never know when life will toss you an obstacle and, chances are, your dog will be with you when it does. OUT can mean the great outdoors as in DO YOU WANT TO GO OUT? We also use it for getting the dog to give up what he has retrieved. In addition, GO OUT by itself means leave this room and go to any other place in the house. For some reason, our hairy linguists never get confused. Yours probably won't either.

14. COOKIE or BISCUIT (Dog biscuit). Some dog owners use the sentence DO YOU WANT A COOKIE? the way I use COME. If you stop training at this point, you'll probably do the same. If not, and bless you, you might want to give Buddy the fun of anticipating a treat. So, when you say DO YOU WANT A COOKIE? or SPEAK FOR A COOKIE, he gets more than a dog biscuit. He gets to salivate a little imagining a dog biscuit.

15. SPEAK (Bark). This essential vocabulary word should be taught verbally and then as a hand signal for safety's sake. When the burglar on the other side of your thin door hears SPEAK, SPEAK, so what? When you point your finger at your dog, unseen by Raffles, and he hears the thunderous roar of your Maltese, he might just turn tail and run away. Even if your dog's voice won't keep you safe from harm, at least he'll be able to SPEAK FOR A COOKIE.

16. TAKE IT (Take this in your mouth). As long as you're going to play with your dog, to toss a ball for him to bring back or to encourage him to carry small packages or help pick up his own toys, you might as well add the phrase for that skill to his vocabulary. TAKE IT is commonly used as a fetch or pick up command. Young puppies love to chase a toy or ball and *sometimes* bring it back. If you keep retrieving fun for the dog, and if you name this activity, you have a

nice game plus the option of tightening play retrieving into the real McCoy (reliable retrieving on command) later on.

17. WAIT (Wait). Some dog owners don't like to use STAY except in the formal sense—the freeze on command. When letting the dog know he is not going on an excursion or not getting out of the car just then, they say WAIT instead of STAY. This can also communicate something important to the dog who is off-leash trained. It would make more sense to say WAIT as your dog bounds toward the corner or toward the exit of the park than to say STAY, which would be asking him to freeze in mid-leap. WAIT tells him not to cross the street, leave the park, rush out the door—until you tell him to. But it allows him to be at ease while waiting. It's worth teaching.

18. OFF (Get off). OFF is the proper word to bellow when you find Buddy eating a greasy bone on your lemon yellow silk couch or shedding in your bed. It's also good for correcting jumping or any other situation in which the dog's big, hairy paws are on something they should be OFF.

You'll probably have your own additions to these important basic vocabulary words. My Shepherd, Scarlet, for example, kisses when you say LIPS and gives her paw on the command GIVE ME FIVE. Once your puppy has learned how to learn vocabulary words and the commands implied in them, he will learn subsequent words quite rapidly. You can even make him bilingual, translating his commands into Spanish, Yiddish or Pig Latin.

VOCABULARY FOR A PET OWNER

Canis familiaris, since he has no verbal language to speak of, still relies on body language, pretty much in the same way he did in the days of Tyrannosaurus rex. With your own high intelligence, remarkable powers of observation and a strong desire not to lose the best of what was, is there any reason you can think of why you couldn't relearn the ancient skills?

Learning your dog's tongue eliminates the chance for much of the misunderstanding between men and dogs. It will enrich

you, as a human, to learn dogspeak. It will enrich your relationship with your dog by leaps and pounces, offering you previously hidden comedy, pathos, information.

Here are the basics. Most, you will be able to understand. Many, you will be able to "speak." Who needs Berlitz!

Dogspeak

1. PLAY BOW: When either stretching after a nap or expressing friendly sociablilty, the dog will assume an elongated position, forelegs on the ground, rump in the air. This stretch position is one of the chief ways your dog invites play. Almost all dogs use and can read this posture, even if it is done awkwardly by a human being.

2. PAWING: Pawing is a submissive, friendly gesture, also used as an invitation to communicate or play. Paw back—and while you're there, tell him SHAKE and you've got an instant trick.

3. PANTING: Your dog pants both to cool his body (because he does not sweat through his skin as people do, but rather via his tongue and the pads of his feet) and to express his friendliness. If you pant back to him, he will either respond in kind or he will translate. That is, he'll either pant back, or he'll play bow, paw at you, wag his tail. Dogspeak, like English, has synonyms.

4. MOBBING: Mobbing and subsequent mouth licking are most often seen in puppies when their mother approaches. Your puppy may mob you when you come home, and for similar reasons. In the wild, and sometimes even in the *tame*, when mother is mobbed and her lips are licked, she regurgitates her half-digested meal for her babes. You, on the other hand, can merely pet Buddy when he mobs you. There's no need to get carried away with this.

5. SUBMISSIVE POSTURING: Submissive posturing begins with the ears back, tail tucked, hind leg up, a roll over onto the back, neck and tummy are exposed, tip of tail is wagged, dog urinates. This is language you should understand since you will be training and correcting your dog. This is not language you should "speak" as it is not appropriate for someone of your species or station.

6. TAIL WAGGING: Tail wagging is an indication of friendliness. If wagged low, it is an indication of submission. When only the tip of the tail wags, your dog is not sure if you will be happy about what he is doing—but he hopes so.
7. TAIL TUCKING: Submission and fear are expresseed with a tucked tail. The female will also tuck her tail to protect herself from amorous males when she is not in season. When ready to mate, she flags her tail, tossing it high and to the side.
8. HACKLES RAISED: The expression, "Don't get your back up," should let you know that raised hackles mean anger. If you see a dog with everything going out and forward— hackles raised, ears forward, tail high, up on his toes— that's an angry dog. Fear is expressed by a pulling in—ears back, tail tucked, rounded back (tummy tucked). Mixed messages—ears back, hackles up—could mean a shy, sharp dog or fear biter. This dog, the one expressing ambivalence, is less predictable and can be more dangerous than the aggressive dog.
9. THE T POSITION: The more dominant of two dogs will form a T by leaning on the submissive dog's back with his muzzle or even his paws.
10. MOUNTING: Mounting is used for mating and also as a display of dominance. A dog wishing to vote himself alpha will mount another dog of either sex as an act of self-assertion. There is no appropriate reason for a dog to be allowed to mount a person.
11. SUBMISSIVE GRIN: This is a caught-in-the-act grin acknowledging submission.
12. LAUGH FACE: An open-mouthed happy look invites play or shows that the dog knows he just cracked a particularly worthwhile joke.
13. MEANINGFUL SOUNDS: As you add the posture to the sound, you will be able to interpret the variety of utterances your dog makes. His voice can express a range of feelings— sadness, boredom, joy, anger, friendliness, pain, a call to gather, a kind of "ahem" to get your attention, loneliness, exuberance.

Encourage eye contact.

You can see what a dog is feeling by looking into his eyes.

TOOLS

Benjamin

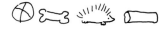

Collars

Show lead for puppies

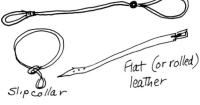

Slip collar

Flat (or rolled) leather

Toys

Bed

Sheepskin
Old towel
Bath mat

Bed should be washable
and portable. Bed
says "home" when
you travel.

Bowls

Stainless steel is best

Comb and Brush

Crate

Order from your local
pet supply outlet.

14. EYE EXPRESSION: You can see what a dog is feeling by looking into his eyes, just as he will know what you are feeling by looking into yours.

Now you have a good idea of how to start your little one off on the road to education and some idea of how to understand his body language and what he'll eventually be able to understand of our language. Illustrated are the tools you'll need to train and care for him. As you'll soon see, his requirements are modest, his tastes simple.

4

Basic Etiquette for Puppies

No animal should ever jump on the dining-room furniture unless absolutely certain that he can hold his own in the conversation.

Fran Lebowitz
Social Studies

ETIQUETTE REFERS to an acceptable mode of social behavior. Unlike commands, which are executed only on order, manners color behavior at all times. Unless you and Buddy still live in a cave, he will need some manners.

Naturally, your pup's mother began this phase of his education, teaching him to play gently, to wait his turn, to hold still for his bath, to greet her with deference, to stay close to home. Now you will continue her good work, housebreaking your pup, helping him to accept your absences, teaching him to walk on a leash, respect your privacy, behave like a gentleman—not a wild animal.

Two aspects of your dog's nature make it possible for you to teach him manners and train him to obey commands. First, he is a pack animal. His pack instincts allow him to respect and revere a strong, clear leader. In fact, his mother gave him a wonderful model for how an alpha dog should conduct herself—with supreme confidence, with courage, with fairness, with intelligence, with final authority, with affection. This is the model that we, too, will use for inspiration in caring for our little pup. If we do not, if we fail to take the upper hand, our pup will become confused and insecure. With no top dog to show the way, he'll try to take that position himself. It's just a natural part of being a dog to be a little pushy when it comes to leadership. But since you would make a better leader for a human plus dog grouping, you must let him know as many times as necessary that the position of leader is taken, thank you. Dogs need not apply.

The second aspect of your dog's nature that makes him a near perfect pet is that he is a den animal with an instinct to keep his sleeping quarters clean. It is this instinct that will allow you to rapidly housebreak your pup. And housebreaking is the natural place to begin his lessons in etiquette.

HOUSEBREAKING

The fact that there are no wild Old English Sheepdogs, Pugs or Beagles doesn't alter your dog's nature as a den animal one drop. So to prevent one drop—on your rug, parquet or linoleum—you are going to housebreak your dog the natural way—by using a crate.

Had your dog been born in the wild, he would have been born and raised in a cave or den. For the first few weeks of his life, his mother would have kept the den immaculate by ingesting her puppies' bodily wastes. Once the little puppies could negotiate the trip, mom would scoot them outside to do their business. You've got to admire her housekeeping.

Soon enough, the little wildlings would get the point, keeping the house clean and sanitary. Mother knows best. After a time, the puppies might even momentarily disappear behind a convenient bush for privacy and neatness' sake. That's housebreaking—in the wild.

Domesticated dogs, such as Old English Sheepdogs, Pugs and Beagles, still behave this way, even when their dens are whelping boxes in breeders' houses. Some breeders even encour-

age their bitches to begin housebreaking the puppies when they are all of six weeks old. They set up quarters for the little dogs with a swinging door that leads to an outdoor area. First the mother teaches the babes how to use the swinging door. After a few trials, the pups learn to get in and out without getting hit in the face by the soft leather or plastic door. Then they begin to copy mom. Dogs are wonderful mimickers. What they see is what they do. In no time, most of the soiling is done out of doors. Even little puppies can appreciate the advantage of keeping the den clean.

Chances are, you will not have an indoor/outdoor set-up with a flexible dog door for your little puppy. Not to worry. Instead, you will purchase and use a wire crate which Buddy will regard as his den. With the possible exception of the first few times he is confined, he will not soil his quarters unless he is ill and can't help it. Of course, understanding his tender age and physical inability to control himself, you will set up a schedule for Buddy that he is able to maintain. Thus, he will learn to keep *his* house clean—just as he would have in the wild. And since you will take him from the crate to the great outdoors before he relieves himself, your house will stay clean, too. By the time he's six months old, he will expand these courtesies to your house without being confined.

With the use of a fair schedule, rigidly adhered to at first, confinement in a crate and lots of praise for using the appropriate toilet area out of doors, your housebreaking program will toddle along pretty smoothly. If you are home, you can use the crate, praise and a schedule from the time your puppy comes home. But if you are out to work all day, you cannot confine the little puppy and hope to find the crate clean when you come home. He just can't wait that long when he's only a few months old. In that case, you'll have to paper train. It's slower and somewhat messier, but what choice do you have? You can't quit your job and you can't force a puppy into bodily control he simply does not have.

You'll still want a crate. Every pup needs a den. Put the crate in a small room or area and paper the rest of the floor. When you're home, praise Buddy for using his papers. If he should goof and use your carpet, it's really not that big a deal. Merely

Even little puppies can appreciate the advantage of keeping the den clean.

The crate will teach your puppy to keep your house clean.

tell him NO, NO and then transport him nonstop to his papers. There, tell him he's terrific. Then clean your carpet thoroughly.

Housebreaking is a necessary, mechanical task. It should not become a battle of wills or any other kind of battle. Don't rub the puppy's nose in excrement. That's disgusting. Don't hit him with rolled-up newspaper. That practice should be as extinct as our early ancestors. There's no need to do anything but show the puppy where to go, praise him for going there and confine him briefly in between walks. Here's how:

Housebreaking Schedule for Young Puppies

7:00	Walk puppy	4:00	Kids (if you don't
	Offer food and		have any, adopt
	water		some) walk puppy
	Walk puppy		and play with
	Puppy plays while		puppy until every-
	you make coffee		one is tired and
	and try to wake up		quiet. If you don't
	Puppy goes into		have kids, you're
	crate to rest		elected.
10:00	Walk puppy		Feed puppy by 5:00
	Puppy plays in		in order to help
	kitchen or den for		him get through
	about fifteen min-		the night dry
	utes at first, then		Walk puppy
	for more and more		Puppy plays with
	time each week		toys in the kitchen
	Puppy goes into		while dinner is
	crate		being prepared
1:00	Feed puppy	7:00	Walk puppy
	Walk puppy		Play with puppy
	Play with puppy in-		Crate puppy
	doors or out	11:00	Walk puppy
	Crate puppy		Crate puppy overnight

Note: The crate can be kept in the kitchen or den during the day and in someone's bedroom at night. Empty, it is easy enough to move around.

If you can't be home to walk your puppy throughout this important early period, then you will crate the puppy on schedule when you are home, playing with him as above *after* walks or after he relieves himself on paper. During the time you are out to work, the crate will be left open and paper will be available for the puppy to use. Plan to get rid of the paper entirely when he's about five months old. You'll be able to see by his behavior exactly when he's ready to wait all day for a walk.

While this period of training is admittedly difficult, it passes. And while I do not consider a dog *capable* of being truly reliable until he is six months old, the dog will get closer and closer to being truly reliable each week. As this happens, there will be fewer accidents, therefore fewer clean-ups and, in general, a more relaxed atmosphere. By the time he's five months old, it'll be safe for you to walk barefooted again. Well, *pretty* safe.

As you see that the puppy can stay out of the crate for longer periods of time without soiling the house, stretch this period of time and, as soon as you reasonably can, begin to cut the number of walks. Very soon, you will be able to feed the puppy before his walk and then walk him. Next you will be able to cut a walk and even out the timing of the rest of the walks, making them, for example, five hours apart. From six months to about eight months, the pup should have four walks a day. From then on, three a day will be his required routine.

Once the job is done, you'll forget it immediately. But, if you rush ahead before the puppy is ready, you won't get it done. In that case, you'll have a chronic mess on your hands. So, please, like mom, be patient. Don't expect the puppy to exercise control he simply can't. Don't get mad at him when he's being the best puppy he's able to be. Also, don't, because you're tired, let the puppy stay in the crate for hours and hours on end. He'll either be forced to soil the crate or be very uncomfortable. He'll also get very, very lonely. In addition, do not let the puppy go out into the fenced yard alone to do his business. It will slow housebreaking and make for many accidents indoors. First of all, you will not be there to praise him. Praise speeds training. Second, you will not be there to know if he relieved himself or

not. Perhaps there was something wonderful to explore and he forgot. Then, when you bring him back indoors, he's no longer distracted and he feels an urgent need to go. Don't fall into the trap of letting him go out unaccompanied and then thinking he's spiteful if he soils the rug right after a "walk."

One additional point: exercise makes the dog need to relieve himself. So, a longer walk, on leash, with you, is usually preferable to a shorter walk or a quick pit stop in the yard. Besides getting the puppy to do everything you might want him to do outdoors, the longer walk will relax you, get you breathing more deeply, strengthen your heart, firm your legs, lift your spirit. Aren't dogs wonderful?

LEASH TRAINING

Leash training shouldn't be any problem at all. Begin it with a follow-the-leader game the first day Buddy is home. Simply follow him. As you trail after him, tell him he's a good puppy. As soon as you can, reverse the "game," getting your little puppy to switch off and follow you for a while. Call to him, teaching him his name at the same time. Whistle, clap, praise, bend down and extend your arms to get him to come to you. Within a week, you and puppy will look like Mary and her lamb, with puppy following you everywhere you go. Now add a light leash. A show lead is a good, reasonably priced interim collar and leash combination for fast growing youngsters. Put the leash on Buddy and follow him wherever he goes, keeping the leash loose. If you are taking Buddy outside from day one, begin with the leash on when outside and play this follow-the-leader game off leash when indoors.

Sometimes your puppy will want to sniff and explore. Good! Let him—and follow him. After about a week, he'll happily walk and follow or walk and be followed on a leash. When you are outdoors, encourage him to follow you the same way you did at home. A tug-of-war won't get him moving if he seems stuck. But if you bend down, extend your arms to the side and use your sweetest voice, he should unstick himself and run right to you.

Begin with a follow-the-leader game.

Now add a light leash.

A tug-of-war won't get him moving.

But if you bend and call him sweetly, he'll run right to you.

Tie the leash to your belt. He'll learn to keep his eye on you.

Now you can add another phase to leash training, one that will have a strong positive effect on the way the dog bonds to you. Once he'll follow you pretty well, after a week or two, tie the leash to your belt and have him accompany you wherever you go at home. He can shadow you while you water the plants, wax the car, prepare the morning waffles. He will become literally and figuratively attached to you, exactly the state of affairs appropriate between man and dog. At first, he may need some encouragement to come along. Give it to him. At any rate, he'll catch on pretty fast that he's tied to you. He'll accept the bond and trot along with you everywhere. Then you can tie him on for longer periods, offering him your close company while you teach him to stay near you, to watch you, to watch out for you. He'll be learning to keep his eye on you. He'll be identifying with you. And when the time comes to call him away from something fascinating, you'll have established a bond he'll be likely to honor.

Of course, you won't keep the pup tied to you all the time. But done occasionally, this exercise will have a positive bonding effect on both master and dog.

Before we hang up our leashes and go on, one more word about them. When your puppy mouths or bites his leash—and he will—stop him. Tell him NO and take the leash out of his mouth without making a game of tug-of-war out of the procedure. If he persists, another NO and a sharp tug upward with the leash will free it from his mouth. The leash should not be used as a toy or tug object, either accidentally or on purpose. It is your tool for training and control, your symbol of authority—not a plaything to be chewed up and discarded.

"TABLE" MANNERS

There are two important aspects of table etiquette for pet dogs. First, the dog must learn to give up his food to you without a squabble. Second, he must learn not to steal food that isn't his. Both aspects of table manners, taught early, will prevent biting over his meal or over a stolen prize later on. Both aspects, also, go *against* the dog's instincts yet are necessary lessons for him when he dwells with human families. While we can communicate in his mother's style even here, we must be clear that she would not correct the puppy for these transgressions. In fact, in the wild, food protection and food stealing would help a dog to survive. When living the domesticated life, dogs must be trained against these instincts or they can become threats to their families.

When you feed Buddy, tell him OK as you place his dish in front of him. Nothing conscious will be getting through for the first week or two. But something is getting absorbed. Your puppy is beginning to learn that you will give permission when he is to eat. After a couple of weeks of this automatic, no-big-deal training, put the bowl down and do not say OK. Do not, in fact, say anything. If your puppy waits (he probably won't), in a couple of seconds tell him OK, GOOD BOY and let him enjoy his food. If on the other hand he goes for the food, gently pull him back with your hands on his collar and tell him NO. You may have to do this a couple of times. Then, when he looks up at you and/or waits just a couple of seconds, tell him OK, GOOD DOG.

Continue the OK at every meal and when giving treats. Practice having the puppy wait for the OK *no more than twice a week* until the puppy knows to wait for the OK. Then you can relax and just continue to tell him OK when you feed him without testing him every week. This is not, and never should be, a contest of wills. Do not use this as a trick to show off to your friends that you have such great control over your little beast that he wouldn't eat a steak unless you told him he could. This is not a trick. It is etiquette. We are intelligently laying the groundwork for teaching Buddy not to steal and not to vacuum up food and trash when in the park or out in the street. We are beginning to prevent him from taking the pizza off the coffee table and lollypops from short children. Do it in the way you remove band-aids—fast, matter of fact, and not too often, please.

After a month or so, your puppy should have no problem waiting for the OK. While you are teaching him restraint, occasionally add food to his dish while he is eating, using your bare hand. If he should growl when your hand comes near his bowl, tell him NOOOO, give him a firm shake by his collar and TAKE AWAY THE FOOD. The message is clear: Dogs who growl at me don't eat at my house! Feed him again at his next regularly scheduled mealtime—and not one minute sooner. Once every other week, when he's in the middle of his meal, call his name to get his attention, say NO and take away his dish. If he accepts this quietly, add a biscuit to his meal and return the dish immediately, saying OK, GOOD BOY. When you see that your puppy allows hands near his bowl, accepts the removal of his food and will wait for his OK, you no longer have to practice these things. You have successfully communicated to your puppy that he does not have to protect his meal as he would have in the wild. Kept intact in human surroundings, this instinct is dangerous. Furthermore, because of your loving care, your puppy doesn't need it.

Now your puppy has the "background" for learning not to steal food meant for his human companions. He already knows, even if it's locked in his subconscious, that when he is not given the OK, what he sees is not what he gets. If he has the opportunity to steal canapes from your coffee table or butter from the kitchen counter and succumbs to temptation, remind him by saying NO. You can even grasp his collar and jerk him back, repeating NOOO. Do not follow up by rewarding him with a tidbit of what he was trying to steal. That would be like catching a bank robber in the act and trying to get him to reform by giving him a bag of quarters! In addition, rewarding your dog for not stealing what's yours in the first place teaches him that if he waits, he'll get your food without stealing it. This will make him the most tenacious, obnoxious beggar since dog and man made their original pact. Instead, we'd like him to understand that some nifty goodies just aren't for him. Period. In return, we will refrain from eating his chow. After all, fair is fair.

While your dog is still immature, try very hard not to leave him alone with temptation. Even if he means well, he'll find it impossible to control his urges very well. Prevention is still the very best kind of dog training, especially with puppies.

TEACHING YOUR PUPPY TO ACCEPT STAYING ALONE

A lot of problems between dogs and people come from how the dog reacts to being left alone. Before we bum rap our little friend, let's remember that he is a pack animal. He was not built to be alone. In the wild, a dog would almost never find himself alone—except, perhaps, if he decided to take a brief, solitary walk around the perimeter of the pack's territory to remark the boundaries. The whole point of the pack is community living— working and playing together, hunting as a group, raising pups together, howling at the moon in chorus. Your dog was made from this same mold. Staying alone does not come naturally to him. With effort, he can adjust.

Be purposeful and sympathetic when training your dog to accept your necessary absences. By your behavior, show him over and over again that you will return to love him, care for him and fulfill his needs. Who else does he have now that he's been domesticated?

Begin by setting up a crate/den area for your puppy, establishing a permanent place for his water bowl and food dish, giving him a washable, old towel to sleep on, papers on which to relieve himself, safe toys to chew. Chewing will help him relieve his anxiety. With that, my friends, he'll be loaded! Keep this in mind if he chews on something of yours one day in an attempt to make himself feel better. It is anxiety, not spite, that makes him do bad things when you're out. Still, you must correct him. But understand that while he can adjust to being alone, it's an unnatural state for him and he's never going to like it.

Your comings and goings during the first few days the puppy is yours will help to communicate to him that you will come and go. Some puppies learn this quickly and adust easily. Some have more problems in this area. Naturally, if your dog was bred to protect a flock, he will tend to get upset when his flock departs. Understanding the qualities bred into your dog for generations will help you to predict how he will react to being left alone, to training, to outings, to children.

Having something to do helps when you're left alone and feeling blue, even for dogs. Your dog should have safe things to chew. In addition, another pet will help ward off lonely feel-

75

Another pet will help ward off lonely feelings.

He was not built to be alone.

Staying alone does not come naturally to him.

ings—another dog or a pet cat. But since you will be the one caring for that other pet, you have to want it, too. If one pet is all you care to have, Buddy will have to adjust to that fact. You can help him feel better by giving him good exercise, particularly right before you leave. That will tire and relax him. He will also have a sense of your fairness. You gave to him. Now he can make a sacrifice for you and wait quietly until you return. You can train him before you leave him for the day. This reminds him that you are his pack leader and reminds him of his security as well as his limits. He will feel less anxious knowing he has a firm, fair, loving leader. You can even give your dog a warm, master-is-at-home feeling by leaving the radio on. Music and voices can be of great comfort to a young puppy who has to spend the day alone.

If you can, don't plan to be gone all day when you first get the puppy. But what about his first night? Even if you are right there, it is his first time away from the comforting warmth of his siblings, the familiar smells of mother, den and breeder, the sounds he heard when his tiny ears first began to hear. Will he be able to feel secure and sleep through the night? Not a chance.

There are two schools of thought on how to cope with the puppy's difficult first night. The first says you should give him a little box, a towel, a ticking clock to remind him of his mother's heartbeat and put him in the kitchen where, when he cries in anguish, your sleep won't be disturbed. I am not of that school and, I hope, neither are you. Pack animals need as much company as they can get. For all his life, your dog should be sleeping in your bedroom. It increases his powerful bond to you. It gives him your comforting presence when it's costing you nothing. It is happily reminiscent of those early days when home was one big stone room with a fire near the open entrance to ward off intruders.

Put your puppy's crate in your bedroom. Give him the towel, the clock if you like, a goodnight kiss. And don't plan to sleep straight through the night. A little lost sleep never killed anyone. If your puppy cries, take him out of the crate and take him to his papers. If he uses them, praise him—but not too much—and put him right back in the crate. He'll probably let

Dogs in bed?? Read on.

you sleep for several hours before his next piercing whine. But, take heart. You are helping a small creature to adjust to the loss of his genetic family and, at the same time, helping him to bond to his new and permanent family. His second night, the little trouper will probably only wake you up half as many times as he did the first night. And so on. After a few nights, Buddy will accept what is and sleep until sunrise. As he gets older, he'll learn to mimic you, watching Johnny Carson and then sleeping in until ten in the morning. If this system appeals, there is one no-no to observe. When your little puppy cries that first night, do not get up and take him into your bed. That particular reward for waking you will guarantee a nightly encore. Better wait until he's older and then you can invite him up when you feel like it and keep him on the floor the rest of the time. More on dogs in bed in the following section, the one on spoiling!

To sum up this important area of puppy education, be considerate, plan ahead, keep your puppy with you when you can and remember he's a pack animal with a powerful leaning toward group living. Finally, keep your departures and arrivals matter of fact rather than hysterical. This will communicate to the puppy that these events are a normal, necessary part of his life with humans.

BONDING, AFFECTION, SPOILING

It doesn't really matter if you spoil Buddy, as long as you train him, too. A trained, spoiled dog makes a pretty nice pet.

Let me explain. Let's say I've spoiled my dog. I've lavished lots of affection on her. I've taken her with me everywhere possible. I've considered her feelings, her welfare in all the major decisions I've made since I got her. I take her on vacation with me, sometimes sacrificing luxury and service in order to find a place, however crude and rustic, that accepts dogs. I've given up wearing white. I order special professional feeds for her and supplement her meals with expensive vitamins, with liver, with cottage cheese. I think about her when I can't be home. Have I left her alone too long? Did I exercise her long enough before I left the house? Can I manage to get back earlier and take her for another walk, a romp, a run? Spoiled? You bet!

On the other hand, if I am eating a succulent steak, licking a cone, crunching a pound of Fritos, I have the choice of whether or not to share with my dog. I may indeed share. But if I don't, she won't bark, whine, jump on me. She won't steal the food. She won't sneak into another room and tear up my best dress in frustration. If company comes and they don't want to play with a German Shepherd, I can tell Scarlet to go lie down and she will. She comes up on the bed when invited—and not otherwise— and if I invite her every morning, still, *the choice is mine.*

If you own a dog and have lost important choices that should be yours, your dog is spoiled and the situation is bad, possibly heading toward red alert. Spoiled dogs can become biting dogs, especially if spoiling means they fancy themselves pack leaders in your house. However, if spoiling means that you enjoy lavishing what most normal people would call excessive amounts of love on your dog, spoil away. If your spoiled dog is trained, you can kiss him all day long and never have a problem. If your spoiled dog is not trained, you might be harboring a boring little tyrant, the kind of dog your friends secretly detest, the kind of dog who is welcome nowhere. A dog should be under your control, should have learned by the time he's half grown to look to you for guidelines, for permissions. You should be able to take your dog almost anywhere unobtrusively. And your dog should be able to be unobtrusive at home—when there's company, when there's good food on the table, when he's left alone, when you're in bed, when you're busy. A trained dog, no matter how much you cater to him, will not become an obnoxious pest. An untrained dog—spoiled and catered to—can easily become a mini-czar, unappeallingly running the lives of otherwise intelligent adults. Train your dog, keep control, remind him occasionally, as his mother would in the wild, that control is yours (a simple sit stay will do the trick) and you can mush away all you like. You can share your Fritos, your bed, your bath if you choose. *If you choose*—that's the key.

Now that this is clear, where should your nice, spoiled dog sleep? Once again, with feeling: Since he's a pack animal with a strong yearning for company, give him an effortless extra eight hours of your time. Bed him down in your room—but not in your bed.

If spoiling means excessive amounts of love, spoil away.

82

Letting a dog sleep in his master's bed gives him the notion that he is an equal. Since that is an illusion, and a dangerous one at that, it's terribly unfair to let him convince himself thus. Of course, you can call the dog onto the bed to cuddle with him. That's one of the pleasures of having a dog. But don't let him spend the night. He has a tendency, as a dog, to get possessive and to try to rise to lead the pack—in this case you. Keeping him in your room will give him company and increase the positive bond between master and dog. Keeping him on the bed often leads to biting, to marking on the bed, to biting the same sex mate (his competition), to fleas in bed. Who needs it?

While loving your dog as much as you like—and sometimes more—keep in mind that he is a pack animal who lives best with a combination of affection plus limits. This is, after all, his own mother's formula. Do not regard your dog as your equal. He isn't. Do not let him regard you as his equal or subordinate. It can only lead to trouble. Try to increase the positive bonding effect by reminding your dog that he is responsible to you, by training and caring for him, by playing and exercising together. Eliminate senseless guilt about not giving him enough attention when you know you do. And let him sleep on the floor and eat dog food. When you're both sure he's just a dog, you'll be free to have more fun.

PROBLEM PREVENTION

If your puppy's mother could have one long talk with you, this would probably be her topic. Who knows better than a mother the importance of keeping the cheekiness of offsprings within limits. Every mother knows that children test, act out and see how far they can go. And every mother knows that the very first place their little darlings like to try out their newfound bravery is right at home. While neither she nor you would want to break the spirit of a zany little puppy or have him behave like an automaton, still you both can see the value of not letting things get out of hand.

Your best weapon is the same as hers. Be a firm pack leader. In the face of strong, intelligent leadership, less problems will arise. Your very attitude will prevent most of them. Adopt mother's stance, understanding the pup's inability to behave as an adult, yet curbing excessive flack even while he's learning. Knowing you have the right and duty to be in charge is a good beginning when it comes to dog problem prevention.

Your puppy is built to look to a strong, loving leader for direction and, as we've said, his mother has already provided a sterling model in his eyes. Now you just have to step into her shoes and continue on—loving, protecting, making rules and setting limits.

The first limit to be set has to do with nipping. Yes, it is perfectly natural for a puppy to put his teeth on everything he can reach and yes, you can and will set limits about what he can and cannot gnaw upon. First of all, he can't gnaw on you. It's easiest and best to be rigid here. His milk teeth are as sharp as needles. But if that's not enough to persuade you, his adult teeth have formidable clout, in some large breeds, hundreds of pounds of pressure per square inch. Having been bitten by both small and large dogs, let me assure you that in neither case is it fun. Even a very nice dog can get overexcited when playing. If the dog has not been taught to keep his teeth off you, he can escalate gentle mouthing to a painful bite in no time. When your puppy nips, tell him NO. If he nips again, tell him NO again, stopping him physically with your hands. This means you can hold him off by his collar. Do not hold his mouth shut. This frustrates him so much that he loses the connection between the nip and the correction in his struggle to get out of your grasp. Better than that, if he keeps at it, grasp his collar and shake him, just the way his mother would have if he took untoward liberties with her. After the shake, if he's still full of beans, put him in his crate to cool off and think it over.

Confining your dog to his crate as a punishment is effective. It will not make him hate his den. After all, when you were a kid and you were acting fresh and obnoxious, you may very well have been sent to your room for a while. Did it make you hate your room? Certainly not. Like you, dogs have a sense of fairness. If your correction is clear, your dog will accept it with equanimity. If you are vague, how can the puppy understand why you are railing at him? He doesn't know what he did

to deserve your wrath. More important, he doesn't know how to avoid it next time.

But if you are clear about what you don't like—nipping, for example—your correction will be understood as follows: "Look, Buddy, I've asked you once, twice, three times not to exercise your sharp, little teeth on my hands. But you refuse to stop. If that's the way you're going to be, I won't play with you for a while. Go sit in your house and think it over!" Of course, you won't want to isolate the puppy for too long. Fifteen or twenty minutes is a long time when you're a kid. But three minutes is so short that it will be forgotten before you can say, "Hey, you're doing it again!" Healthy, loved puppies are very forgiving creatures. Correct fairly and your puppy will both learn and continue to adore you. He will not hate you for exercising your right to teach and lead.

You are, in fact, going to use the crate not only as den and bedroom, but as your chief tool for prevention of dog problems and one of your chief methods of correction. We have just discussed the specific message the puppy understood by being confined for a while after nipping. In general, use of the crate lets him know that he cannot behave in certain ways in your house. The crate, on the other hand, is *his* house. You should respect that fact, too, and let him be when he's in it. Do not continue to explain to him in great detail why he's a rotten specimen and why you should have gotten the puppy with the black spot over his eye instead. Leave him alone. On his own, he will use his crate when he wants peace and quiet. He'll go in it to rest, to get away from your children, to avoid being mauled by company, to juice up when he's feeling burned out. So when he's not in the crate, keep the door open and let his house remain accessible. Keep it clean, washing it out once in a while or vacuuming out the hair. When you clean house, put his toys in his crate. That gives a strong, positive message, too—this space is yours. When you think about it, there isn't too much a puppy can call his own. But your Buddy is rich. He has his own room, which can be transported from your bedroom to the kitchen to the den—and even taken on vacation.

When your puppy is small, you won't expect him to be

perfect all the time. Neither can you overwhelm him by correcting everything at once. Instead, concentrate on the more serious behavior problems, working with them as they crop up. Besides curbing his nipping, you will want to prevent destructive chewing by crating him when you aren't home or when you can't watch him. At the same time, when you can watch him, you can begin to let him know what he can chew and what he can't by monitoring his behavior in a very easygoing fashion. He may even start out on his Nylabone and move, quite accidentally, to the molding. Simply move him back to his bone. Tap the molding he was biting with your hand, saying, "NOOOO," and offer him the bone again, saying, "OK—Goood dog." Be hawk-like in your observations but patient as you correct. (That's mother's way.) After all, he doesn't know better until you show him. And, in fact, he won't really know better until you show him many, many times. He really needs the repetition and consistency to learn. Plus, he needs to mature both physically and mentally before you count on him to be reliably well behaved when you leave him alone. The training can't work miracles. He will still have to grow up. Naturally, training helps things proceed in the right direction. If you simply wait for the puppy to outgrow the chewing stage, you might find yourself paying off a new couch while you wait. Training speeds the dog's understanding of what you want and what you don't want. Maturity is what enables him to remember the training with reliability and to pocket his anxiety when he is alone. The young puppy cannot do that. So when he must be left, the crate is the only sensible answer.

The third puppy problem you'll want to work with early on, if it comes up, is excessive barking. Again, all you can do when he's really little is lay some worthwhile groundwork. Working in an appropriately low-key fashion, when your puppy overdoes it in the noise department, tell him ENOUGH. If that warning doesn't quiet him, repeat it once more as you give one firm tug on his collar. In addition to this, you must give him an outlet for his voice. All creatures need to express themselves vocally, with the possible exception of giraffes. Your dog has a right to vocalize and you have a right to limit his right. That is, your dog needs some time and perhaps some place where it's perfectly okay for him to make noise. And you have the right not to let him do that noise making at three in the morning. In order to give him an outlet for his voice, in addition to letting him have time to run around and bark outdoors, teach him to SPEAK on command. (Instructions for this are in Chapter 10, "Games to Play with Your Dog.") Once he will do this, he will focus more of his barking on you and you can play voice games with him outdoors or when his noise won't bother family members or your neighbors. This will make it easier for him to respond to ENOUGH when his barking is inappropriate or when it goes on for too long.

One more problem deserves some space here rather than in a future chapter on correcting chronic adult problems because when it occurs, it should be stopped quickly and not allowed to last until your dog is full grown. This is the unpleasant problem of coprophagy or stool eating. Some puppies indulge in this habit out of boredom. Some get the habit after being punished for a housebreaking accident. They seem to be trying to get rid of the evidence of wrongdoing. And while most people find this habit unnatural, it isn't really. When your dog was a little puppy, his mother kept the den clean by ingesting the feces of all her puppies. If your bitch is bred, she, too, will keep her puppies clean and healthy by ingesting all their wastes. Still, when you pick up your little puppy to kiss him, you'd prefer his breath to smell like milk. Moreover, by ingesting feces, he can reinfest himself with the very parasites you have been battling to get rid of. If he does this with the stools of other dogs, he can infest himself with whatever worms they might have. The only way to break this habit is to clean up immediately after your dog evacuates. When he's outside, keep him on leash and do not let him sniff the droppings of other dogs. This habit may take a few weeks to break, especially if your puppy is using papers while you are out to work. But by keeping things as clean as possible, you will end the habit soon enough. Try not to freak out when your pup "cleans up" by himself. This too shall pass.

In all training, particularly in problem prevention and correction, it's important to examine the activity from the dog's side, too. Sometimes you'll feel that what the dog wants is unacceptable. That is certainly the case with biting. Other times you'll feel that what the dog wants to do would be fine if you had some control over it. This is the case with barking. By pausing to look at life momentarily through dog-colored glasses you will see which activities you should stop cold and which you can redirect. That is intelligent, humane dog training.

"It's called *heeling*."

5

Basic Obedience Training

If you think education is expensive,
try ignorance.

Derek Bok

MOST PEOPLE THINK of basic obedience training for dogs as a series of commands that the dog, reluctantly, learns to execute. On one level, this is accurate. However, before we begin the mechanics of teaching specific commands, let us look for a moment beyond training as the dog learning a series of orders. Underneath it all, the very important lesson your dog is learning is that he must do *what* you tell him to, *where* you tell him to do it, *when* you tell him to do it and *for as long as* you say he should do it.

Many dogs are trained in the sense that they will respond mechanically to certain words but they have not gotten this all-important message. Without the message, training can resemble a series of tricks that the dog performs, much as an arcade pigeon will "dance" in the hopes of getting a kernel of corn. With the mesage, the dog works. He knows more than just what position to assume with his physical form when he hears a command. He understands your position as alpha dog. He enjoys his role as educated dog. His appearance is intelligent and alert. In no way does he resemble a dancing chicken.

We will train our dogs to that deeper level where they work with grace, where one command can flow into the next with ease and understanding. By using the natural training techniques in this book, you will learn how to teach Buddy the mechanical response to a verbal or nonverbal command and, in addition, you will learn how to tell if he is humoring you or really getting trained and how to move training into the realm of education. If you think education is expensive, you're right. It will cost you time. But the results will be worth it because you will have much more than an obedient dog. You will have, for your efforts, the dog you long for—one who obeys you in a cheerful, reliable manner, one who comes when called under any and all circumstances, one who merits run of the house, one who offers you rich, fascinating companionship and the deep pleasure of real communication and rapport with a fellow being who happens to be of another species. The SIT STAY, which follows, is not merely a command to teach your dog. It is the first of many steps toward this larger goal.

SIT

Begin training your puppy indoors without distractions. As he learns his lessons, move outdoors where distractions abound. To start, the pup should be wearing a flat or rolled leather collar. Keep the leash handy, but begin with it off.

If a little puppy tried to look at something dangling over his head, he'd have to sit to keep his balance. So, in order to teach your puppy to sit, hold a ball, squeak toy, jingly set of keys above his head—or simply snap your fingers gaily—while you say SIT. If your puppy does not sit in order to look at your hand, you can gently seat him by placing one hand lightly on his rump and the other hand under his chin. Now gently lift his head and lower his rump as if he were looking up at your hand in the first place, saying SIT as you do. Immediately, but calmly, praise the puppy and tell him OK, which means he can get up. He will already know OK because you have been using it with food and outings. If the puppy does not move when you say OK (some won't) back

Hold a toy above his head and say SIT.

Practice sit both on and off leash.

up and call him to you by crouching and extending your arms out to the side. Praise him when he comes.

Now repeat the command SIT, trying once again to get the puppy to look up at your hand and seat himself. It may be a matter of holding the object in just the right spot to get the puppy to sit. When he does, praise him well and release him with OK. Try this a few more times, having the puppy sit in a different spot each time. To end your session, tell him OK and play his favorite game with him or take him for an outing.

Practice the sit, both on and off leash, twice a day for a few minutes at a time. At the end of a week, your puppy should sit most of the time when you say SIT. Of course, he may pop right up again. To prevent quick exits, STAY will be the next command.

STAY

Now when you begin, put your puppy on leash. Work in a quiet area without distractions. Tell your puppy SIT and when he does, tell him STAAAY. As you elongate the command, dropping your voice at the end so that it doesn't sound like STAAAY?, swing your flat open hand toward the puppy, palm facing him as if you were going to touch his nose with it. Stop short of touching him and withdraw your hand. This is the helpful hand signal that goes with the stay command. Now step back one step and wait.

The point of training is to help the puppy to learn things, to get them right and to feel satisfaction from doing so. It is not to trick the puppy into making a mistake so that you can correct him. Unfortunately, when many people train, it looks as if that is what they think training is all about. Perhaps they remember too many surprise quizzes and mean teachers.

We don't want to be mean teachers to our darling puppies. So we will wait thirty seconds and, if the puppy does not break, we will tell him OK, encourage him to move toward us and praise him when he gets there. But it will be only the unusual or temporarily dazzled puppy who won't move on the STAY at first. When you think about it, how could an untrained puppy know what this word or any other word means until he is

Tell him STAY.

Swing your open hand toward the puppy—

stopping short of touching him.

97

shown. So when you command STAY and your little puppy gets up and walks toward you, don't be angry, disappointed or frustrated. Don't think he's stupid or spiteful. Simply, kindly, firmly, patiently say NO, walk him back to exactly where he was sitting, tell him SIT, signal him and tell him STAY and once again back up one step and wait. If now your little Buddy stays and on top of that has the light of intelligence in his large, brown eyes, wait a moment (let's say sixty seconds at most), break him with an OK and praise warmly, but not hysterically.

Early on, like maybe the first time you try a SIT STAY, your puppy may catch on that STAY means just that and he may want to get comfortable. He'll lie down. Almost every puppy will do this on the SIT STAY at the very point he figures out what STAY means. You could be so thrilled he's staying that you do nothing. Wrong! Lying down on a SIT STAY means your puppy is breaking a command. If he can lie down, he can leave. He either obeys you or he doesn't. And while in your heart of hearts you don't really care if he sits or lies down to stay on the living room rug, to the puppy, this is a test of your leadership. He knows that if you fail to correct his breaking of this command, he can break any and all others. So, when your pup lies down on the SIT STAY, say NO, SIT, STAY, enforcing each command with the leash. That is, NO tells him he did wrong to lie down, SIT tells him what he should be doing instead, especially as you pull straight up on the leash and seat him again, and STAY repeats and reenforces the second half of the command he is working on. As many times as he breaks by lying down or getting up, patiently repeat the three words, NO, SIT, STAY and place him back where he was sitting in the first place. This is his method for testing out truths, for testing limits, for learning exact definitions of vocabulary words. He's not being bad. He's just learning like a dog. What more could you expect of him?

Once the battle of the slouch is over, after you tell him STAY begin to get farther away from him until you are waiting at the end of your six-foot leash. Do not at this time drop the leash or work without it. For now, slower is faster. A good foundation will speed training over the long haul.

As your little puppy begins to understand the definition of

If he breaks, tell him NO—

SIT—

STAY!

Now, back away.

He must stay—

no matter what!

STAY, by doing, you'll want to gradually lengthen the time he will stay without breaking. Do this erratically, having him stay one minute one time, three minutes the next time and twenty seconds the third time. Your unpredictability will make the puppy watch you more carefully because he will not be able to second guess your timing. That's good.

Also, as your puppy gets more reliable on the SIT STAY, you'll want to teach him that he should STAY even in the face of distractions. So after a few days, practice not in the quiet room but in the kitchen while dinner is being prepared, out front when kids are playing in the street, here and there on walks—on quiet streets, on busy corners, gradually building his ability to stay longer and to stay despite passing buses, kids, dogs. At first, you may notice that your puppy does not generalize. It's as if he is thinking, "You mean I have to do this *outside*, too?"and "You mean I have to do this even when there's a cat in sight?" Eventually, after four or five or six levels of exposure, he will begin to generalize. Once he learns that he must stay in the face of tempting children and other dogs, on noisy, busy streets, inside stores and on elevators, he will begin to understand that he must stay when you say so, no matter what. He will even begin to look less intense when he's staying because he knows that he shouldn't even plan anything until he hears you say OK. And that's good, too.

COME WHEN CALLED

Of course your little puppy comes when you call him. It's only natural. You're his pack, his mother figure, his alpha dog, his guru. Moreover, his umbilical cord, the psychological one, is still attached. He wants you around, in sight, close to him. He can't wait to get to you and be cuddled in your arms. So why are there so many owners calling out into the dark from dimly lit porches, "Fluffy, come. Fluffy, where *are* you? Fluffy come home." Why are there so many owners running past you in the park shouting, "Did you see a large black dog with a white blaze on his chest pass this way?" Because umbilical cords don't last (they're not meant to), but training does.

You will want to do everything possible to bond your little Buddy to you, to encourage him to come and then love him up for doing so, to keep the command COME pleasant and inviting, to teach games in which the puppy fetches and *comes*, swims and *comes*, runs and *comes*, hides and *comes*. But when all is said and done, you will have to formally teach your dog to come, first on leash and finally off leash. If you don't, if you think because he comes so quickly when he's small that he'll do it when he's tall, you might end up late at night scouring the neighborhood with a flashlight saying, "Did you see a small white shaggy dog pass this way?"

It is a natural stage in maturing for the dog to become a bit defiant and to test like mad. Think *teen-ager*. If you've been one, if you have one, if you know one, you know what I mean. Sometimes, during puppy adolescence, it's not the particular issue that counts, it's that there is an issue, any issue. Remember that dogs are lovable but consummate con artists and this is the age when this skill blooms. There is no real mystery to it. It happens at the onset of sexual maturity, easily recognizable in the male dog because it is the time shortly after his testicles descend, around the time he begins to lift his leg and mark everything in sight. It is then, at about eight or nine months of age, that most dogs get very assertive and try out for top dog. It is then that your sweet, pliable puppy may not come when called, that is, if you don't train him.

Beginning when your puppy is brand new, crouch down, open your arms wide and call him in. Now you can exercise the instinct that sent you out to find a dog—kiss, kiss, hug, hug. Continue to call him, using his name and the word COME—BUDDY, COME—whenever there's an obvious treat in store (hugs, a walk, dinner, a ball game). If there's something you guess he won't like—a bath, for example—don't call him to come for it. He won't, and you'll be teaching him that he doesn't have to come when you call him. In those cases, go get him. The same, of course, is true if you have to reprimand him. *Never, never* call your puppy to come to you for punishment. Even his mother wouldn't do that. She'd go and get him and let him have it. So will you.

Once the puppy is trained, then you can call him whenever you need him and follow up with a correction if he does not come. Still—never call him to come for punishment. If he's bad,

Open your arms and call him in.

Then kiss, kiss, hug, hug.

go get him, take him to the scene of his crime and then tell him how rotten he is.

Once your puppy has learned SIT and STAY pretty well—but not necessarily engraved in stone—you can put him on leash, begin with a SIT STAY, proceed to the end of the six-foot leash and then turn around and call him to come. If he's confused by the stay, repeat the command COME in a sweet, singsong, appealing voice and give a little tug toward you with the leash. Or repeat, BUDDY, COME and run backwards. Either method will get him moving toward you. Ask him to SIT when he gets close enough for you to touch him. Now bend and reward him with some friendly head scratching and some warm, kind words. Now you can begin again, doing a couple of SIT STAYS that end in recalls and then one or two that end in OK. If you practice a certain pattern over and over again, your dog will begin to anticipate your command and break before you give him the word. This makes for poor training. Remember: You call the shots. So when you practice something new and want to try it a few more times, mix in the old work in random order. It will make your pup listen better.

Add the COME to your daily practice with your puppy. Make sure he sits in front of you *before* you praise him. This will prevent him from sideswiping you when you call him and he's a cocky teen-ager. You know the routine. You call your dog. He races at you full tilt. Just as you reach out for him, he swerves and departs. You get up, brush off your clothes, curse him under your breath and say, "Did you see a chunky, tan dog with a red collar pass this way?" Not our Buddy.

Now if you call your dog to the bath and he doesn't come, or if he doesn't come at any other time (except for facing up to a blob on the rug or a chewed shoe, because on those unhappy occasions you'll go and fetch him), you will go and find him, snap on his lead, say COME, COME, COME in as pleasant a voice as you can muster, and back up, the dog following along, to the very place you were standing when you first said, BUDDY, COME! Get it? It translates: When I call you to come, you come to where I am. Your dog will get it, especially since when you get to where you were, you're going to do another five minutes of

Proceed to the end of the leash—

and call him to come.

Good dog!

SIT STAY—COME. Now, for sure, he's got the all-important message. He understands that when you call him he must go to you and that if he doesn't, you will bore him to death by practicing the recall until he's blue in the face. Of course, we said five minutes the first time. As he gets older and bolder and if he ever doesn't come out in the park or yard, then you will repeat SIT, STAY and COME over and over again about twenty times. It sounds boring, I know. It is. And that's just how your dog will feel. It will make it not worth it for him *not* to come, an important concept for dogs to learn.

Since the recall is such an important command, as you practice it, you can add an exercise to your practice. This will add zest and variety to your sessions. Sometimes call your dog and as he begins to come to you, run backwards for a few feet, then stop, he'll sit, now praise. This will speed up his recall and make it more fun for him to come. Fun is fine. It in no way changes the fact that he *must* come when called, even on those occasions when more fun is in another direction. Work outside on come, keeping your puppy on leash. Praise him always when he comes—even when you are doing a fifteen minute repeat session because he didn't come. In that way you'll be telling him that, yes, he must come, but he will always, always be happy he did so.

This practice will give the puppy a good grounding in this essential basic command. In future chapters, we will add exercises to prepare him for a solid, reliable off-leash recall and finally do the recall without the leash. In this way, should the occasion arise on purpose or accident, your mature, assertive, loose dog will come when called—no matter what.

DOWN STAY

Many trainers and owners favor the COME over the DOWN. But it seems to me that when it comes to life-saving ability, DOWN is the command that has the edge. Picture your dog running out across the road. If you say COME and if he's well trained, he will make a turn, putting himself farther away from you—and farther out into traffic—as he arcs around to return. Suppose, on the other hand, you see him chasing a squirrel that has headed for the road. You shout DOWN. Trained, he will drop on the spot. He will not continue into traffic to turn about. He will not do anything until you get there on trembling legs to take him home. Of course, you'll want your dog to come quickly when called. But give the DOWN command a place of importance in your curriculum, too. Here are the other fringe benefits of DOWN:

- You can reenforce your alpha position (and you should) by requiring your dog to do a long DOWN (one hour) every day. No. That's not a typing error. That's one hour.
- You can calm a dog when company comes by putting him on a fifteen-minute DOWN STAY right after they arrive.
- You can read this book at the vet's office by having your dog on a DOWN STAY while you wait your turn.
- You can have your dog's company—when you are dining, watching TV, visiting, driving the car, nursing the baby, waxing the floor—by using the DOWN STAY if his behavior or the situation warrants it.
- And, of course, you can save your dog's life with the emergency DOWN—a special exercise designed to teach the dog to drop fast on command should the occasion call for it.

For now, we're going to teach a little puppy to lie down. This is much easier than teaching a big dog to lie down because DOWN puts the dog in a submissive, vulnerable position. For this reason, puppy or dog, begin this command at home, indoors. Ask your puppy to SIT. Now pat the floor—actually tap it and make a sound with your open hand, palm down—and say DOOOWN, dropping your voice to give the puppy the looow feeling of the exercise. Some puppies, young ones in particular, will simply lie down to sniff your hand. If yours does, praise him and pet him so that he relates good feelings to lying down when told. If your puppy looks at your hand but does not lie down, place your other hand behind his forelegs and draw the legs

Pat the floor—

say DOWN—

pat the puppy.

gently forward, repeating DOOOWN, GOOOOD PUPPY. Pat the puppy as he stays lying down.

When your puppy seems steady or comfortable, tell him STAY and get up and back up a foot or so. Don't make this a marathon, but break him with OK and praise him warmly. Two to four DOWNS the first day are sufficient. Slow dog training is faster than fast dog training.

Continue to practice the DOWN STAY, adding it to your regular twice-a-day training routine (regular as of this moment) and shuffling it in with SIT STAY and COME. Working indoors on the DOWN, you will probably not need the leash. But if you do, use it. The leash may make your puppy feel more serious and businesslike. Fine. Put it on and let it hang or hold it, whatever works for you. When you say STAY and back up, you can pick up the leash handle and take it with you. Your puppy may work better on leash. Of course, when you begin to practice DOWN outside, the puppy must be on leash so that he will not run away or just fool around. But don't start doing DOWN outdoors until he is very comfortable about doing it on his own inside. Once he will lie down most of the time without the physical assist of pulling his legs forward, you can try the DOWN outside. You may have to start from scratch. Don't let that bother you. This time around it will go faster. However, the first few times you try, he may not want to lie down outside. Assist him and then make your STAYS brief until he gets used to doing this command anywhere with relative ease.

Indoors, you can start to increase the time of the DOWN STAY erratically. One time, have the STAY last five minutes, the next time one minute, the next time try twelve minutes. Do not break the dog because you see he is starting to get restless or starting to get up. He will know that he is controlling the training if you do break him on his clues—so decide ahead of time the length of the STAY and stick to it! He can do it. After all, if he gets tired or bored, he can fall asleep. In fact, many puppies do. In that case, do not go off and write the great American novel. Wake him by gently tapping your foot on the floor or rapping on the door lightly. In other words, wake him but do not startle him. In this way, he'll open his eyes but stay on

Sometimes you have to start from scratch by pulling his legs gently forward.

Good Buddy!

command. Then you can break him with OK and praise him when he gets up.

Sometimes while you are practicing with Buddy, walk around and then carefully step over him while he stays lying down. If he jumps up, correct him by getting him back on the DOWN STAY. Now, step over him again—slowly. This will get him used to being stepped over. This is important because you will find that wherever you want to walk, your dog will be lying across your path. That's just how dogs are.

HEEL

Heeling is usually the first command taught to dogs, which makes a difficult task even more difficult. When your dog is heeling, he is keeping his body in a certain position in relation to your body (which is moving) and he is moving forward at the same time. When you think about it from the learner's point of view, it is easy to recognize that the concept of heeling is more difficult to comprehend than that of SIT STAY, DOWN or COME. Therefore, if you give the dog some grounding with a few other commands and if you teach him how to learn before he learns to heel, heeling will be less of a problem to teach.

When teaching your dog to heel, you'll probably have to start outdoors. Even if you have a small dog and lots of space indoors, heeling is a pretty silly thing to do inside. And most dogs can see that this is so. However, there's no reason why you can't start out in a fairly quiet outdoor spot and, as your dog catches on, gradually begin to work him around distractions.

Start with a SIT STAY, which will tell your dog that he is going to work. Now call your dog to your left side, guiding him with his leash, and ask him to SIT again. This is the heel position: the dog is sitting at your left side, facing straight ahead, his head and shoulders even with your hip. You are both now ready to begin. But take a moment (and make this a habit) to check and make sure your dog is sitting straight. If he is not, when you start to walk forward, your dog will either cross in front of you and trip you, or, if he is pointed away from you, he may not even notice that you have started without him. Having him sit straight inspires him to pay attention. And it looks so

This is the heel position.

Begin on your left leg.

If Buddy lags, tug and release with the leash.

Do not work with a tight leash.

classy, too. So if he sits crooked, take the time to straighten him each and every time you practice the heel. This does not mean he must sit like a soldier, back erect, head up, knees pulled in tight. It merely means he is facing the same way you are so that when you begin to walk, you and your dog will be parallel.

In addition, since the dog is so naturally atuned to body language, you are going to cue him by beginning to walk on your left leg, the leg closest to him. You will also move your left leg last, taking a full step with the right and closing up with the left. In this way, the dog will not only follow the word HEEL, but he will follow your left leg, the one he can see better since it is closer to him. To reenforce this, from now on when you leave your dog on a STAY, leave by moving your right leg first. In this case, since the dog will not be with you, it does not matter which leg you move last when you stop. Here's how it goes: When your dog is moving along with you, start and stop on the left leg and when your dog is remaining behind, leave him there moving your right leg first. Like his mother, you will make good use of body language while you teach.

Beginning with your left leg, walk forward, saying BUDDY, HEEL. Walk at a nice, brisk pace. If your dog remains seated or lags at any time, tug and release with the leash, repeating the command HEEL. By the same token, if the dog forges ahead, jerk him back and then release the leash, saying HEEL or NO, HEEL as you make the correction. Save his name for positive reenforcement and attention getting as in BUDDY, HEEL or BUDDY, COME. Do not work with a tight leash, forcing the dog to remain at your side. It is better to jerk and release, even ten times in a row, than to work tight. The dog learns by trial and error. If you force him to stay in the heel position, he will never learn to assume it on his own on a loose leash. This, of course, is one of our goals.

You'll probably do better at this if you understand that for at least fifteen minutes, you are going to look like a real jerk. The dog doesn't have the faintest idea what you want. The only way to let him know is to physically put him back at heel every time he deviates from that position. When correcting him, jerk the leash so that you actually move your dog's front feet back to the

116

place they should be. Do not merely tug away at his neck. This is merely annoying without being constructive; it does not tell the dog where he should walk. As you correct, also sweeten the work by patting your left leg, talking to him, praising him for each and every step taken without the need for a correction. This gives the dog a range of hints and corrections. It adds variety and zest to your teaching. It will make you look less cruel to your neighbors. But no matter how good a teacher you are, until he gets it, you'll be a foolish looking pair. Then, miraculously, within that first lesson, he'll understand. You'll still have to remind him frequently, for about two or three weeks of practice, but the frantic jerking and the clumsiness will fall away and you'll start to resemble a team. So what if you don't look like Fred and Ginger the first day. Soon enough, you'll work with grace.

Now, as if you didn't have enough to worry about, when you stop, not only must you make sure you move your left leg last, but your dog must sit. At first, tell him SIT. Praise him when he does. But this sit is supposed to be automatic. By the end of your first week of daily practice, if not sooner, your dog should start to sit without being reminded whenever you stop walking. Always praise him for doing so by saying GOOD DOG in your warmest voice and leaning down and hugging him against your leg. You do this by swinging your arm around his left side and back onto his chest. Now, squeeze. Hugging him against your leg reenforces the heel position as well as the automatic sit, which inspired the hug in the first place.

Don't expect your heeling team to work smoothly right away or even all the time. This is as good a place as any to tell you that dogs have good days and bad days. Sound familiar? If your dog is having a bad day, he may still execute a near perfect SIT STAY. But he may be too distracted to heel well. That doesn't mean you shouldn't practice. But you might want to cut your practice short this time. Be sure, though, to end on a positive note by doing something your dog will do well even on his bad days. Lessons should end sweetly so that both of you will want to get back to work again the following day.

Of course, if your dog is having a bad day every day, there's

When you stop, your dog must sit.

Good dog!

something wrong in your training program. First, think about his mother. No, she would never teach her puppy to heel. But if she were teaching him something, she'd be clear, she'd be loving when he got it right, she'd be patient, she wouldn't shrug her shoulders and quit in the middle, she wouldn't make excuses (it's hot, it's cold, it's Tuesday) and if she had to correct him, she'd be fair, swift, more often than not physical, and then she'd be forgiving. Can you say the same for yourself? If you can, check out these additional points. Are you working long enough? You should practice for at least a half an hour a day. If you work (and who doesn't?), practice ten minutes on your dog's morning walk after he has relieved himself and twenty minutes on his evening walk (also after he's relieved himself.) Once a week or so, work for forty-five minutes or an hour at one shot. Even a five-month-old pup can handle it if given a rest in the middle. Now, also, ask yourself if your expectations are high enough. He who expects his dumb dog to do badly will not be disappointed. I know I can get any dog to work happily for me and often when I take a student's dog in class, the dog will work better for me right away. He can read my attitude—and he does. Alpha, he reads. Mom, he reads. Be good, he reads. Your dog can read your attitude—and he can fulfill it, too. He is not dumb. He can learn to work beautifully, no matter what his breed. It's only a matter of time until he heels well. Be patient and keep working.

If you have passed the above criteria and your dog is still having seven bad days a week, perhaps you are not attentive when you train. Your dog will know this, too, and if you don't pay attention to his work, he won't pay attention to it either. Why should he? But if you do give him thirty minutes a day of your full attention, you'll end up with a trained dog and thirty minutes a day in which you don't have to think about your bills, your taxes, your love life, your mother. Training your dog can clear your mind and can help put your problems in perspective.

When you are out working, teaching your dog the virtues of heeling, sprinkle in all his other commands. It will give the work variety. It will teach your dog to make smooth transitions between commands, that which will make him look like an intelligent, working creature and not a puppet. This magic

Two dogs?

Teach them separately, then work them as a team.

120

usually happens about five weeks along in the training. That's the time when many dogs seem to understand the larger picture, when things click. However, your dog may get the point in four weeks—or in eight. Don't worry about it. Just enjoy it when you see it happen. At that point, when he's attentive without reminders, when he'll heel with few corrections, when he sits automatically whenever you stop, when he executes his commands on verbal cue without additional manipulation, continue to practice, occasionally pushing the time so that he learns to work for a longer period without a break. Also, intersperse play with your training. And, when you're safely indoors and at home, begin some of his off leash puppy work. By now, he's coming along so well that nothing could stop you!

ENOUGH

ENOUGH is one of the most peculiar, subtle, necessary things you will ever teach your dog. It means exactly what it says—enough. This is the word that will stop an activity when it is precisely the time to do so, that is, after it was OK and before it gets to be too much.

In order to teach ENOUGH, wait until your dog is on the verge of going too far with something. Let's pretend Buddy heard something at the door. He runs to the door, listens, sniffs, begins to bark. You feel protected. You decide it wasn't so bad after all that you got a dog. Then you begin to wonder if that great cold chicken is still in the refrigerator. Then you decide you don't want to know because you have to lose seven pounds anyway. Then you notice that your dog is *still* barking. By now the squirrel or burglar that started him off is long gone. By now what you need isn't cold chicken, it's aspirin. It's time for ENOUGH.

In your most assertive tone (deep, resonant, not overly loud) say, BUDDY, ENOUGH. If you are lucky, Buddy will turn and look at you with a question in his lovely, hazel eyes. This is the time to quickly praise him. After all, when he turned to look at you, he stopped barking, didn't he? If he resumes his wall of noise, repeat your command ENOUGH! and again praise him if

he's attentive and/or quiet. If, on the other hand, your Buddy is a yapper, a frenetic barker, a noise polluter, a mammoth mouth, you will have to get up, go to the door, grasp his collar and bring him up short with one good shake and the word ENOUGH. Now praise him. And head back to the couch.

Hark. Buddy is giving tongue before you're half way back to the newspaper. Turn quickly back to him. This time when you say ENOUGH, give him three or four shakes. Now march him back to the couch with you. There, put him on a DOWN STAY, plan on twenty minutes and finish the crossword puzzle, occasionally checking to make sure your consummate con artist has not sneaked away.

ENOUGH is indispensable in a variety of situations. When you are gently roughhousing with your dog and you don't feel like playing anymore or he escalates active play into too-rough play by mouthing or biting, tell him ENOUGH and stop the play. If necessary, grab him and hold him until he looks into your eloquent eyes, which are repeating the all important message of the moment—ENOUGH. You can even use the word when playing fetch, when offering treats, when on an outing. Your dog will learn, fairly quickly, that ENOUGH means that whatever was happening was OK but for the time being it's going to stop. Remember to differentiate in your own mind between NO, which means whatever you are doing is forbidden now and always, and ENOUGH, which is used to stop a positive activity before it gets to be too much of a good thing.

Enough said?

STAND

STAND is one of the basic commands that the American Kennel Club requires for its Companion Dog degree. Formally, it is called Stand for Examination and your dog must not move a toe while the judge goes over his body. Of course, the dog who tries to bite or shy away during this exercise, exhibiting bad temperament instead of good training, will not get a leg toward his degree.

At first glance, the STAND does not seem a necessary command for pet dogs. You may, indeed, decide to skip it. But before you do, here's what you can use it for if you decide to teach it. The STAND is a wonderful piece of vocabulary to have when you want to brush or bathe your dog. (So is the command TURN AROUND, which can be taught even more easily than the STAND.) STAND is nice when you want to cancel out the automatic sit—on rainy days, when there's mud underfoot, when it's too cold for a dog to sit outdoors. And you may want your dog to stand for examination informally. If he's shy of strangers, not well socialized or skittish, having people handle him and pet him while he remains standing still is one of the exercises that will help him overcome his shyness. It's also nice for picture taking. And it's easy to teach.

Get your dog onto his feet any way you can; lift him, start him heeling, place your hand under his belly, saying STAND, and exert a mild pressure upward. Work in a quiet room, without the TV or stereo blasting. Be gentle and soothing. Above all, when your dog sits again, do not yell NOOOO, STAND. In fact, if your dog were standing and you yelled, the very first thing he'd do would be to sit or crouch. Once you get your dog standing, you can pet him or brush him, keeping one hand under his belly and repeating the command STAAAND in a soothing tone. Try this routine for five minutes a day, using the time to groom your dog, pet him, sing to him. A great time to work on this is right after you come back from an outdoor training session. In a week's time, Buddy will happily stand on the floor and maybe even in the bathtub.

BONUS: Now that your puppy will stand on command, next time you brush him, when you finish one side, tell him TURN AROUND and gently swing him around with your hands so that his head ends up where his tail was and vise versa. Now, telling him, GOOD DOG, SMART DOG, brush his far side.

There are other obvious bonuses to training your pup. As you can already see, the more you teach him, the faster he can learn. Once he has the basics down pat, many new commands, games and tricks will be learned almost automatically. And even the complex activities that take time will take less time. In addition, the more your dog learns, the more mutual pleasure there will be in the whole education process. The key to it all is to

The stand is also nice for picture taking.

125

systematically teach him how to learn. Then anything is possible.

Note: Do not let the dog merely walk away when you are finished brushing him. Instead, break his STAND STAY, as any command, with an OK and praise.

WAIT

WAIT is a handy command to teach your puppy, especially if you are planning to work him all the way through to reliable off-leash capability. In that case, there will be times when you'll want him to "wait up," but not necessarily to freeze (STAY). STAY would not, at those times, be the right command. In addition, there will be many other times when he will be in a rush to have something or do something. WAIT will be the word to tell him that he can indeed have what he wants, but not immediately. Since dogs live so marvelously in the here and now, WAIT not only adds an interesting, useful word to their vocabularies, it adds a concept that, when you think about it, is pretty hard for a dog to understand. Yet, your dog can understand the meaning of the word WAIT on a short-term basis. That in itself should give strong motivation for reexamining our primitive understanding of canine intelligence.

WAIT, like ENOUGH, is taught by tone of voice. Remember that this was one of his mother's most effective training devices. Thus he is well prepared to understand your tone and to respond to it. Here's how this kind of training works. Your dog is a pack animal. You are his pack leader. He looks to you for direction and approval. If he is doing something, anything at all, and you utter a word, any word at all, in a moderately disapproving tone, he will stop what he's doing because of your disapproval. Now, when you want your dog to wait at the bottom of the steps leading out of the park and you say WAIT (seriously, not angrily), a trained dog (which yours is) will turn and look at you. When you say GOOOOD DOG—he is waiting, isn't he?—he will begin to catch on. If he continues up the steps, say NO, WAIT. *Ah Ha!* he thinks. *Wait means stop.* In that sense, it would seem that ENOUGH would do the trick. Aside from the fact that it would sound inappropriate to *your* ear, ENOUGH

126

WAIT is taught by tone of voice.

really means we're going to stop this activity for now. WAIT means a momentary pause. In the case of the dog waiting to leave the park, jump into the car, join you on the bed, WAIT lets him in on the joy of anticipation. It lets him know that if he pauses for the briefest moment, he can then continue whatever it is he was doing—and that in stopping and starting again (both on command), he has your approval. It's a pretty good deal when you think about it.

You can use WAIT when you are putting your pup's food down on the floor. But only make him wait for a second, long enough for you to get out of the way before he pounces on his dinner. He can WAIT to go out the door (followed by OK, of course), he can WAIT to get out of the car, he can WAIT for you to go first through doorways and down flights of steps. WAIT must be followed by the release word OK to let him know it's OK with you for him to resume the activity at hand. Most importantly, when he's off leash, WAIT will be one of several safety commands you can use to monitor your best friend and keep him safe from potential harm. Add it to the rest of his work. He's worth it.

In fact, to make sure he's around for you to protect, prevent him from running out the door by using the release word OK whenever you take him out. If he should ever try to bolt out or sneak out, tell him NO—WAIT. Then when you are ready to walk him and his leash is safely clipped onto his collar, follow the WAIT with a cheerful OK.

GO LIE DOWN

For some clients, the ones who really seemed to need it badly, I'd teach the GO LIE DOWN at the tail end of my training course. Inevitably they would tell me it was their favorite command. The GO LIE DOWN is your *no pest insurance*. It not only tells the dog to assume a reclining position, it tells him to do it elsewhere. Even for pathological dogs adorers such as myself, the GO LIE DOWN is a blessing.

When you are feeding the baby, painting a picture, stripping paint off an antique commode, making love, checking the souffle, paying the bills, having a fight, talking on the phone, reading a thriller, drinking hot coffee, practicing yoga, stretching for your run, watching the final episode of a twelve part mini-series, flossing your teeth, writing a best seller, GO LIE DOWN is the command you need to send your overly affectionate pesty dog someplace else. *Do not feel guilty* if you do not want to dote on your dog every time he asks you to. You' re a busy person and he has nothing else to do but be a pain in the neck. So, if he's just had his walk, he's eaten well, you've exercised him, trained him, played with him, GO LIE DOWN is a humane, handy answer to your own personal dog pollution problem.

Put your dog on leash. Now point toward a corner of the room you two are in. Tell him brightly (he might as well think this is going to be fun!), GO LIE DOWN. Now, run like mad with him to where you were pointing, repeating GO LIE DOWN, GOOOOD BOY with a final DOWN as you pat the floor in the corner of the room.

Now, pat your dog's hairy head, but don't get amorous or mushy. Go across the room and sit down. If he stays (after all he may just be in shock from your exuberance), after a minute or two tell him OK, GOOD BOY. You can even pet him when he approaches you. Now repeat the exercise about two more times, varying the few minutes he stays.

Each day, try two or three exuberant GO LIE DOWNS. Work in different rooms so that he will do this no matter where you are. This is preferable to the command GO TO PLACE or GO TO YOUR BED because you will want to use this in places where your dog is and his bed isn't. The nicest thing about this command is that it is portable. When you go visiting and your dear Buddy is acting the fool, he can and will and should do a GO LIE DOWN in someone else's house. Flexible is always better. However, if you like GO TO YOUR BED (We do!), teach that, too. Once Buddy has learned GO LIE DOWN, you should be able to translate it to GO TO YOUR BED in five minutes or less. Use the first when anywhere away from his bed and the second only when you are in the same room with Buddy's bed. Asking him to trek through the entire house and up a flight of stairs to go to bed is asking a bit much, don't you think?

What happens if your obedience trained dog lies down on

Go to *your* bed!

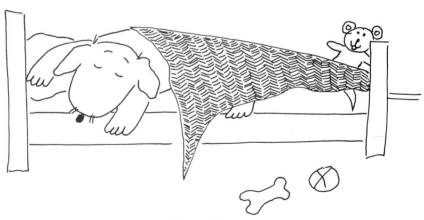

Gooood dog!

130

the spot when you say GO LIE DOWN? Some people would find that funny. They'd realize that when the dog heard DOWN, he ignored the other strange words and just obeyed the command he had already learned. They'd be tickled pink that the training was going so well. Not you! You know better. You want it all. So you will calmly say, NO—GO LIE DOWN, taking the dog by his collar and transporting him against his will to the far side of the room, the side you pointed to. If your dog makes this mistake early on, it is a genuine misunderstanding that you can and will correct without taking it personally and with patience. After all, he's allowed to learn. However, if your dog is already doing the GO LIE DOWN and *then* when you say it he lies down at your feet, beats his tail on the floor and pastes his ears back, he's acting. He is using passive assertion to get his way instead of doing your bidding. Don't be mad. He can't help it if years of selective breeding made him smart, assertive, witty. He's just a dog. Dogs are built to try to rise to the leadership of their packs. Some dogs take the obvious, aggressive route to the top. Others are more subtle in their attempts. In either case, it is not a personal affront. Nor is it to be accepted. It is part of being a pet owner that you look at your dog, think about his behavior, understand him, love him and, once again, remind him of the limits you have set for him.

In fact, the GO LIE DOWN, aside from being terribly useful, is another wonderful, nonviolent way to remind your dog of the dominant position you inherited from his mother. *Benevolent, but alpha* her teaching told him. Yours can, too.

OFF

OFF is probably what you'd say anyway without this book if your dog jumped up on you or if you found him eating pizza on your bed. OFF is the word to use when your dog or part of your dog is ON something you want him OFF.

You can begin to teach OFF by tone of voice. In some cases, particularly in those when your dog has previously been warned not to do something, your annoyed tone and the word OFF will get your point across. But when it comes to jumping on you, the pleasure is so great for the dog that a word alone will not cure the problem. In the case of jumping, you'll have to slip your hand into his collar and pull him OFF you sideways, being careful to get him to the ground gruffly but without causing him harm. In other words, move him. Don't toss him. After much repetition and total consistency, your dog will stop jumping up on you. If he doesn't, turn to Chapter 7, "Trouble Shooting," for more help. In the meantime, be content with OFF. If nothing else, it's a good beginning. And even if you let your dog sleep on your bed, you may need OFF once in a while just so you can give him clean sheets!

6

Off-Leash Puppy

*Better a lie that heals than a truth
that wounds.*

Czech proverb

WHEN TRAINING A DOG to work on leash,
first the dog must learn how to learn. He must learn to listen, to
concentrate, to differentiate, to obey. He learns patience. He
learns to love the act of learning. Next, he is learning skills. He
learns to do things, some of which he does without being told
when he feels like it, and some of which he may not ever do if
you don't teach him how. Once he has learned how to learn and
he has learned some skills, in order to move the level of his
training from superficial to deep, you must begin to push. One
way to push for better learning is to work with an old command
that he has already mastered and increase the amount of time he
must do it. One day ask for a thirty-minute DOWN, the next
day a five-minute DOWN, the next day a one-minute DOWN,
the next day a forty-minute DOWN. Do not push the time by
asking for a little more each day. That would be predictable and
boring for the dog. You should try very hard not to be a dull
teacher. It impedes learning.

Another way to push the dog into a deeper level of learning
is to increase the distractions under which he must learn and
perform. Therefore, if he does a super SIT STAY in your living
room, try him on your block, in the shopping center, on a busy

Off leash is a horse of another color.

street corner, in front of playing children, in the presence of other dogs. Now he's cooking. Now he really understands the meaning of SIT STAY. This is how dogs get trained really well *on leash*.

Off leash is a horse of another color. It is ten times harder. It takes more concentration on the part of both owner and dog. It will teach you patience you thought to be nothing short of saintly. It is also one hundred times more rewarding than on-leash work, the work on which it is based. Because it is more fun and more rewarding does not mean you can skip on-leash work and go straight to off-leash work. That would be like building a house without a foundation. You must have excellent on-leash obedience before proceeding to off-leash work at all.

In addition to all this, the principle behind teaching off-leash work is somewhat different. In on-leash work, you want to push the dog, gradually, unpredictably, to see how well he'll work and to use his breaking as a way to show him that he must work longer, concentrate better and obey, no matter what. His breaking and being put back on command is an important part of how and why he learns. In off-leash work, the opposite is true— and this holds for puppies as well as for dogs. In off-leash work, you want to ease the dog slowly into doing exactly the right thing for longer periods of time. By rushing ahead, even slowly, so that the dog cannot deliver the off-leash skill you want, he learns he can get up and walk away. After all, there is no leash. In this way, all off-leash work is a lie. You must convince the dog that you have the ultimate power to correct and control even without the leash. In order to do this, you must work very slowly. You must be patient. You must forego being a wise guy. You must concentrate like a brain surgeon. And you must work only until the point *before* which the dog will break.

The reason to work so well and so carefully is that taking the leash off your dog outdoors is always a risk. When your dog is fully matured and fully trained, under certain circumstances, you may wish to take this calculated risk in order to let him play in the park or perhaps even heel smartly down the boulevard, right at your side. Under no circumstances, short of six-foot chain link fencing with a locked gate, will you want to take any kind of chance with your precious puppy. He is too immature to

135

concentrate reliably. He is too easily distracted by things that look appealing enough to chase. He is even apt to get spooked by a large truck or a loud noise he's never heard before. He might even experience a surprising surge of assertiveness and take off just to see what you'll do. Until all these issues are resolved by maturity and advanced training, your prime concern is your dog's safety. What then is an off-leash puppy?

An off-leash puppy is a lie. But it's a very, very good lie—a lie, as the proverb says, that heals. In order to improve your puppy's training, to have fun with him and to give him more of the excellent grounding he needs to do safe, reliable off-leash work outdoors in the real world, you are going to do fake off-leash work with him indoors—and even outdoors in a completely safe locale. The work is *fake* because even when the puppy is off leash, he is still contained by walls or fences. But the puppy is very gullible. He won't really know that he's not capable of being trusted where he might get harmed. He'll not only enjoy learning to work off-leash, he'll feel incredibly proud of himself. Does he know the difference between working on leash and working off leash? Ask him to heel without a leash (indoors!) and find out.

By gradually fooling your puppy into a higher level of training, you are giving him practice at being a grown up while protecting him as the vulnerable babe he is. Off-leash puppy training sets the stage most beautifully for the goal of this book—an off-leash dog. Within the safety and quiet of your own living room and with your puppy's collar on but no leash, ask your puppy to SIT and then, using the hand signal, tell him to STAY. Now step back and wait no more than one minute. Now, bend down, extend your arms to the side and warmly call your puppy into them. Praise. Your little puppy has just worked off leash!

Now after you play with your puppy for a minute or so, ask him to SIT again. This time, pat the floor and say DOWN. When he lies down, tell him, GOOD DOG, STAAAY. Back up just a few feet and wait. After two minutes, bend, extend your arms and call him to you. Pet and praise. Play his favorite game. End your first off-leash lesson.

This sort of low key, safe, gentle off-leash training can be done with puppies under five months of age! You will begin the puppy with his grounding of basic commands on leash, and, as you are going forward with his on-leash outdoor work, you can begin his off-leash indoor work, sprinkling it on top of your outdoor sessions like so much powdered sugar for both you and the puppy. Here, in fact, is a sample lesson.

Put leash and collar on puppy and take him out for a walk. Let him pull, sniff, relieve himself. Praise. Put puppy in heel position, sitting straight at your left side. Tell him to heel and practice heeling with the automatic sit for ten minutes. Now, on a quiet side street, practice the sit stay, the come and sit front, the stand stay. If your puppy is good at the down stay indoors, try a short one outdoors. Heel another five minutes. Tell your puppy, OK, GOOOOD DOG and let him sniff, pull and maybe relieve himself again. Now you can take your puppy home. When you get indoors, don't take off his collar and leash just yet. First, put him on a sit stay. While he's staying, unsnap the leash and remind him once more to STAAY. Back up. Wait a minute. Release him with an OK. Crouch and extend your arms and hug and praise him.

Now walk your puppy to another spot or another room and try a down stay. This time you can work him for two minutes. If he should break, take him back to the spot by holding his collar, repeat DOWN, STAY and leave him. Then break him and praise. Never, never, never break him because he is starting to break anyway. He will know that you did that and your training program will be badly harmed. That is not what is meant by working until just before he breaks. Working until before he breaks means that you are watching and aware. It means that you can, as time goes by, see the difference between faking and genuine loss of the ability to concentrate and work. Then you will do one last fun thing and quit for the day. But any dog can do a two- or three-minute down stay. So if you quickly mutter OK as your dog starts to pop up from the down or lift his rump when he's supposed to be on a sit stay, you are fooling no one—least of all your dog. Sadly, he'll be the one to eventually pay for your mistake. His training will not be reliable if you "cheat" so that he "looks good." And then when you need the training to be absolutely reliable so that you can use it to save your dog's life, it

If at first you don't succeed—

try again. Good puppy!

won't be there. Do not cheat.

Now, back to the drawing board. Your puppy has broken and been put gently, firmly back on command in the exact spot he was in in the first place. Now you have released him from the down (when he was staying, not breaking) and you have praised him. Do a sit stay and a recall. Praise and play. You have just finished your second off-leash puppy lesson. Bravo both of you!

Next time you want to work off leash, try a change of pace. It will keep both you and your puppy excited about training. This time teach him an off-leash game. Take your puppy and a box of dog biscuits into your living room. Put your puppy on a sit stay, off leash and, holding a biscuit right up to his nose for a split second, say SMELL IT. If he tries to grab it, the little pig, say NO and move it away. You have already taught him he can't have food without permission, so don't take his greed personally. Just remind him with NO. Then place the biscuit six feet in front of him, well within sight. Wait one hippopotamus. Now, with wild enthusiasm, say OK, FIND IT—and as he eats it—GOOOOD DOG.

What if your little garbage can won't wait? The hand is faster than the mouth. Save the cookie. Don't allow him that tasty reenforcement unless he does the job properly. Instead, tell him NO, SIT, STAY, making sure that the sit stay is done exactly on the spot where he began. Start from scratch. SMELL IT. One hippopotamus. FIND IT—GOOD DOG. Even a slow-witted puppy finds out pronto the virtues of playing SMELL IT, FIND IT by the rules. Here they are:

- The joy of working off leash
- The joy of eating a biscuit *and* getting praised for doing so
- The fun of a "find"
- Approval and attention

Will your dog love this game? You bet he will. Now look at it from the trainer's point of view. While you are having fun, you are reenforcing tight off-leash work in a safe setting. Your puppy learns pretty fast that if he wants the damn cookie, he better wait. Therefore, whether he knows it or not, he's getting off-leash trained. Yet you are not ruining his obedience work

Play *Smell it, Find it*—with a leash—

and without a leash.

with food rewards because this is clearly a game and you will not use biscuits or cheese balls when you are training him. In addition, the cookie will gradually move farther and farther away from your puppy. By the end of one week of playing SMELL IT, FIND IT you will be placing the biscuit near the doorway out of the room. In addition, your puppy will be able to wait three hippopotamuses. By the end of the second week (go slowly, my friend), the puppy will be leaving the living room to search for the cookie. So, within a month or so, your puppy will not only have this fun reenforcement of an important command, but he will be doing fun scent work. As you play, slowly make the finds harder. But if your puppy can't find the biscuit or gives up, know that it's your own fault. You went too fast for him. Backtrack and make the finds easier for him again. The only way to keep him working longer and make him able to achieve more difficult finds is by building his confidence ever so slowly and carefully. Eventually he will search up (on tables, bookshelves, couches), he will search under (pillows, couches, newspapers) and he will search in (finding cookies stuffed into your pocket or hidden under your shirt). So rush forward slowly with your scent dog and when he's truly hooked, replace the cookie with one of his favorite toys, adding to his vocabulary and his skills by having him smell and find rubber balls, knotted socks, squeaking frogs. In fact, if you had one lying around, he might search for an old pterodactyl bone, for nostalgia's sake. He can be sentimental, too.

Continue to sprinkle five or ten minutes of serious and playful off-leash work into your training sessions, making sure that the puppy has exercised before his off-leash lesson and that his off-leash work is done indoors where he cannot get into danger if he breaks. Thinking ahead, you'll want to play and invent games that reenforce all the commands, particularly the recall. Here are some good puppy games that reenforce come when called in a speedy, accurate, immediate fashion.

Puppy in the Middle: You and another family member (or friend) can call the puppy back and forth between you in a gamelike, fun way that will make him feel silly and joyful while he's obeying an important command. You can both crouch and extend your arms, calling the puppy one at a time. Give the

Puppy, come!

Come,
come,
come!

Goooood puppy!

143

other person just long enough to touch and praise the puppy and then call him to you. Instead of a formal, BUDDY, COME, you can call PUPPY, PUPPY, PUPPY or COME, COME, COME. You will still reenforce this command, even being informal. Do not use food. Of course, SMELL IT, FIND IT does, but that is because food is part of the game, not a reward per se. Even there, when you can, replace the food with a nonedible object, using the biscuit occasionally as a special treat after the game has been learned. Here, your praise and attention are reward enough. Play this puppy in the middle recall game when your puppy is full of energy and wanting to race anyhow. He'll love it.

Hide and Seek: Call your puppy to come and then run away and hide. First, Buddy sees you calling him. Then you begin to race through the house, calling COME, COME, COME, with Buddy in hot pursuit. As you can see, having a puppy lets you act like a carefree fool. Isn't it great! Run until you are out of breath with puppy chasing and getting egged on with COME, COME, COME. Then, at the last minute, turn around and crouch and let him catch you! Praise and hug and roll on the floor. Now try it again. You and puppy will both be using your energy constructively, reenforcing a quick, exciting, joyful off-leash recall, getting to know each other better, and having a ball. Not bad.

Each day, after an on-leash practice session outdoors with your student prince, try one, two or three of his commands indoors off leash. Then end your session with a game, preferably one that lets him practice what you preach. Here's another sample off-leash lesson.

After outdoor work, bring your puppy home and have him do a sit stay indoors. While he's staying, snap off his leash, reminding him only one more time to STAY. If he breaks, take his collar in hand, walk him back to the same spot and repeat, SIT STAY. Don't be angry. It won't help him learn.

Break him this time by approaching him and saying DOWN. He should go straight from the sit stay to a down stay. Tell him STAY once and back off. Try sitting in a chair. This makes you smaller in the dog's eyes and therefore less alpha. Therefore, your sitting may make the dog break. If it does, this gives you another level of training to work on. Tell him NO. WALK him back to the same spot. Tell him DOWN. Tell him

Try a down stay.

STAY. Now, sit again. If he stays, after two or three minutes, pat your legs and tell him OK, GOOD DOG and let him come for his praise. You can even take five and toss a ball for him. In fact, let's do just that.

Take your puppy's favorite ball and toss it for him to retrieve. With warm enthusiasm, tell him TAKE IT, GOOD BOY, TAKE THE BALL. He probably will. Dogs love to chase moving objects. Now don't rush at him to get the ball back. Wait for him to bring it to you or encourage him to do so. It's his treasure. Let him enjoy it first—chew on it, bat it around, carry it about. When he wants you to toss it again, he'll approach. But many puppies still won't let go. Tell him OUT and gently take the ball. Now toss it for him again so that he sees the reward in bringing the ball back to you. As he gets hooked on this retrieving game, you can toss the ball saying TAKE IT and then call him to COME, GOOD BOY, COME. When he arrives, tell him OUT and throw the ball in another direction. Don't beat this game or any other game to death, though. If your little dog returns the ball to you a few times and then wants to play with it by himself, let him. If you want to get back to his lesson, get up, go to him, tell him OUT, take the ball and put it away. Now you can resume obedience work. Here is an important lesson in itself. Eventually the dog must learn that training is for your convenience and that he must obey you not just for thirty minutes during a formal lesson but whenever and wherever you judge it to be necessary or convenient to issue a command.

What of the concrete-mouthed dog who won't give up the ball? (Your dog, right?) Place your hand over his muzzle, exert some pressure so that you are pressing his cheeks against his teeth and tell him OUT. He'll give you the ball. And you may not have to repeat yourself too many times. Always praise your dog when you get your way—even if you got it by force.

Playing at retrieving is something all owners do with their dogs, but many fail to add communication and education to their fun. Adding words to go along with the action does not spoil the fun. In fact, it's more off-leash work on your puppy's part and all within an atmosphere of pleasure.

In addition, when you give words to your puppy's skills, you are setting the stage to expand upon those skills later, to reuse

146

them in other games. Here's another off-leash game that reenforces several skills and commands and, like retrieving, offers good exercise to the puppy. These games are great, too, for rainy days when you don't want to play with Buddy outside.

Take a spare bookshelf or board and use it to block a much used doorway. Now when your puppy wants to follow you, he'll have to go over the board. Use the word OVER as his command to jump. Most dogs get a great kick out of jumping and low jumps are safe for most puppies. Of course, he shouldn't take off from or land on a slippery surface. He always needs good footing for jumping and landing. And keep the jump very low. You won't want to raise the height until he's mature and his muscles are strong, his bones tough, his adolescent awkwardness over.

The first few times over some puppies will need an assist. You can use the leash, run with him toward the board and give him a little boost to help him sail over the low board. Then praise and go back the other way. Once he likes the jumping, you can cross the board and call him to come, slipping in the command OVER as he approaches the board. It won't seem like work, but it is. And he's doing it off leash, too.

Now it's time to go hunting. You will hunt not with an elephant gun and a long line of local bearers, but with your eyes and ears. What you are hunting for is a perfectly safe place in which to train your puppy off leash outdoors. The only perfectly safe place is an area that it totally fenced. No matter how good your puppy seems to be, he is not reliable. If you trust him to act like an adult, you may be worse than disappointed. You may lose him altogether.

But if there's a fenced school yard, tennis court, parking lot or backyard with a gate that closes and latches, you can begin to practice off-leash puppy work outdoors. In this case, after a warm-up elsewhere and then in the fenced area, going over each of the basic commands on leash, you can begin to test them all out off leash.

Don't rush to try heeling, though if your puppy is really attentive and seems to thrive on off-leash work, you may try it soon. You are better off trying static commands such as the sit stay, stand stay and down stay first. They are easier for the puppy to do. Once still, there is an inertia that tends to keep the

147

Static commands such as the sit stay—

and the down stay are easier for the puppy than heeling.

148

STAAY.

Three months old and working off leash! *Good* puppy!

puppy there. Once moving there is the tendency to keep moving, often not in the particular direction or style you have in mind. It's easier, in other words, to take off when you are on your feet and moving anyhow.

Keep fairly close to your puppy when you begin to work in the outdoor fenced area. Although he'll figure out the fence and know he's not *free* in the world, still, there are smells that will entice him to forget about work. There are birds and squirrels moving about. There are leaves falling and new odors that need identification and investigation. There is the richness of cool earth beneath his feet and suddenly it may seem like a good idea to dig a hole. Or he may just want to roll on the grass, looking up at the bluest of skies and letting his mind wander freely among the clouds. Unfortunately, none of these activities is part of your curriculum—at least not just yet. So if you keep the distance between you and the puppy short, you'll be able to move in quickly and gracefully when it's necessary to make a correction.

Understanding that working outdoors off leash is a new level for him, you know in advance that you will be doing a lot of correcting. So be it. You know this is natural and you have no reason to be angry, impatient, frustrated. Once Buddy catches on to the big news of the day—that he must even work outdoors and off leash, and even when he'd rather not—he'll accept the inevitable and do his commands. He may even enjoy himself. The first day, keep your requirements brief so that he has the experience of success, and you do, too. Then plan to lengthen the time you both work in your fenced area gradually over the next few weeks.

Once you have tested the sit stay, down stay, stand stay and the come, off leash and outdoors, by all means release your puppy with an OK and praise and let him sniff around, roll around, count the clouds. Find a comfortable log to sit on and enjoy watching your puppy being a dog. You may wonder why he's doing the things he's doing and if so, good for you. The more you understand your dog, the more you'll enjoy him and the more of the canine good life you can offer him. His basic motives are similar to yours—curiosity, pleasure, a desire to learn about his environment, a need to test his strength and courage, a drive to exercise wit and humor. In addition, he carries instincts different from ours. He may roll in something ghastly, forcing you to rush him home and into the tub. Dogs seem to love to cover themselves in pungent odors, perhaps from the time when it would have served as a good disguise during the hunt. And dogs love to dig. Sometimes they dig to find a cooler spot on which to take a nap. They also dig to bury bones and food, making a kind of primitive canine pantry. You may see your dog rubbing back and forth against a tree or some bushes giving himself a good scratching and leaving his scent there at the same time.

In addition, dogs love to use their mouths, as babies do, to investigate things they find. First, they will find out if the object is edible. If not, it may turn out to be fun to chew. Some dogs like shredding and will spend hours with sticks, toys or even the Sunday paper, happily making confetti. This nest-making instinct is very natural for dogs and seems to give them great oral satisfaction. For the average dog, shredding is a prime way to pass a lazy afternoon. For the average unspayed female, shredding may be your first clue that she is coming into season. If your dog shreds and spits and the objects being shredded are not your stocks and bonds, shredding is a harmless hobby. But if your dog swallows what he shreds, you must find him nonshred-dable chew toys. Any veterinarian will tell you endless horror stories about the things he has removed surgically from pet dogs, an experience both dog and owner will do well to avoid. So don't let your pup get into the habit of ingesting nondigestibles.

Your puppy may just enjoy his break by racing an imaginary partner or following a scent you cannot pick up. Freedom to be a dog and do as he will, within reason, is one of the great rewards of off-leash work. So it is fitting that he be given a taste of it after his off-leash lesson. Again, the fence is latched. The puppy is safe. He has earned his free time. Our expectations of him are high—but not unreasonable or ridiculous.

Once the puppy is accustomed to working in this fenced area, you may want to try off-leash heeling, just for a few feet. Of course, if your puppy's on-leash heeling is not excellent, you can easily guess how successful his off-leash work will be! So be sure that before you try this, your puppy is really heeling with his leash held. This means when you say BUDDY, HEEL, Buddy walks at your left side and sits automatically when you stop. If every few steps require a correction or if Buddy drifts out of position with great, predictable regularity, he is not ready for off-leash heeling.

In that case, since we are not in a contest to see who can train his puppy first, you can stick to your on-leash heeling for a few more weeks until the puppy seems to get it. Heeling is a complex procedure and goes slowly.

When your puppy is heeling so well on leash that you sometimes can forget he's there, you and he are ready to recheck the latch on the gate and try a few minutes of off-leash heeling. You will work up until a point before which the puppy will break. This may be three steps the first day. I cannot emphasize strongly enough the need to proceed slowly and the importance of not pushing the puppy into needing a correction in these early stages. Of course, you may try this for a mere minute and your puppy may get it all wrong. In that case, you will have to do two things. You will have to make a clear, gentle correction. Then you will have to return to on-leash work, for that session and for another few weeks before trying the off-leash heel.

Your first attempt goes something like this: Heel the puppy around the inside of the fenced area on leash in the normal fashion, praising for good work. When he is warmed up, simply support the leash with your open left hand and let the balance of it fall behind and drag on the ground. If your puppy begins to lag or take off, all you have to do is close your hand on the leash and make a correction. If your puppy, perhaps not even aware of the difference, heels as usual, the few minutes of heeling in this way will begin to get him used to a different feel on the leash, an important first step in the long off-leash process. After a few moments, praise, hold the leash normally and work for another few minutes before quitting for the day. This was a banner moment. Be sure you and your puppy celebrate with a favorite game.

If your first off-leash heeling session goes well—the puppy is attentive and trying hard, and you feel comfortable with that small but important diminution of control—try again the next day. In fact, for a minute or two, literally, after other work and

Support the leash with your open hand and let the balance of it fall behind and drag on the ground.

play, work your puppy drop-line fashion, letting the leash lie across your palm and then drag on the ground. Any time the puppy lags or drifts off or tries to escape, merely close your hand over the leash and make a normal correction. After you do so, do not open it again but instead hold the leash as you would for on-leash work. You may, after a few minutes of regular heeling, give the puppy just one more try at beginning drop-line work and then, after one or two minutes, stop, have him sit (remind him if necessary), praise him warmly and play a game you both enjoy.

Some owners, when training their puppies, have a tendency when things are going really well to go on and on. They want to try just one more down stay, just one more lap with the drop line, just one more recall. Often this attitude means they work until the puppy loses the ability to concentrate and makes a bad mistake. Then, instead of ending on a bright note, they end the lesson on a sour note. Or, instead of ending on a bright note with energy left for a refreshing game, they feel the need to work even longer in the hope of returning once more to that bright spot they ruined. There is always tomorrow. The puppy is yours—and you are his—for keeps. If you get a few minutes of good work on something new and, from the puppy's point of view, something difficult, that is the time to quit. Then, when it's time to work again, both you and your puppy will feel that you are returning to resume something pleasurable and interesting. If you push beyond, if you go for just one more this and one more that, neither of you will feel thrilled at the anticipation of another practice and learning session. In fact, with that attitude, you may push the puppy into mistakes one day and not train again for days at a time. In dog training, slower is faster.

After a week of moments of heeling with the leash draped over your palm, you may want to try to start the off-leash section of your practice session that way and then just turn your hand over and drop the leash as you are walking. If you feel butterflies in your stomach, good for you. That means you have the insight and sensitivity to understand that this small act is a huge step. Of course, the area is fenced and the gate is latched. In addition, if your puppy tries to bolt and run away, you can swiftly move your foot and step hard onto the dragging leash.

Now work with the leash
dropped and dragging,
but—

if your puppy tries to run away, swiftly step hard onto the dragging leash.

So you are doubly insured against losing your dog, figuratively and literally. Still, as your hand turns over, as the leash falls silently through space, you and your puppy are entering an exciting new level of training. Much more important, before the leash even lands on the grass, you and your puppy are entering an exciting new level of communication, contact and understanding. The communion between dog and owner when the leash is not held is tenfold what it is when you are holding the leash and can safely let your mind wander.

The plain fact is that starting from this moment, the moment you turn over your hand, your full attention must be on your puppy. No longer can you indulge in daydreaming while training your dog. If you do and the leash is on the ground or, later on, off the puppy, the puppy will feel the loss of your attention to the exact degree that you remove it and his behavior will imitate exactly the loss he feels. That is, if you watch him but are also thinking about something else, his work will be a little off, just about as much off as your mind is off him. Remember, he doesn't have verbal or written language to rely on. His feelings are intact. He knows how he feels—and how you do. If you look the other way and forget about him, even for a moment, he may drift away entirely. He's a pack animal. Testing is his forte. He knows what's going on on a gut level and he responds to it as if it were the gospel, as, indeed, it is.

With your concentration happily on your puppy, you can now work with the leash draped over your hand and then dropped. Again, do this after a regular on-leash session elsewhere and then a warm-up of off-leash sits, stays, downs and comes in your fenced haven. Off-leash puppy work is still a lie—after all, the fence is there—but oh, you kid! Just look at the two of you now!

You probably won't want to go beyond working the heel with your drop line dropped while your dog is still young. Even though all seems to be going well, he's still a growing pup and easily distracted. At this point, if you snapped off the leash and said HEEL, chances are too strong that he'd forget all about you and go his own way. Anyway, there's so much else to do with him that it will be easy to let his off-leash work wait until he is a

Oh, you kid! Look at the two of you now!

dog and has, for the most part, put his puppy ways aside. Since when it comes to play, we never want him to put the engaging ways of youth aside, let's end our off-leash puppy chapter with one more off-leash game, one that uses his obedience training, one that educates, fascinates, elevates.

This game is a jumping game. Since you have taught your puppy OVER and he likes to jump, now you can set up an obstacle course for him that requires him to go over several very low jumps in a row. If you want to get fancy, you can set it up so that he goes over some things and through others. An old tire makes a nice, solid hoop for a dog to go through and this obstacle, combined with a few boards to jump over, makes a nice activity for owner and dog. In addition to the fun of learning the course and using it, it is more than good exercise for your pup. Learning to overcome obstacles, both literal and figurative ones, builds his confidence, making him a more flexible, easy going, well-adjusted animal.

Since you have already taught your small gamesdog to jump over a board, that part of the obstacle course will be no problem for either of you. You can leash him and jump the boards with him to psyche him up for this new adventure. Later on, you can wait at the far end of the course and cheer him on, coaching him with OVER, GOOD DOG, COME, OVER, GOOOOD DOG. If your tire hoops present a problem (some dogs don't like the overhead part of a hoop until they try it a few times and discover it won't bite), you can place the puppy on one side and call him through from the other. Use the sit stay to prevent him from following you around to the other side. In this case, since it is a game and not serious training, you can start the puppy going through the tire for a food reward. But your applause and petting will replace the tidbit the very first day on the course. Like mom, keep the flow of learning moving. Don't let the puppy's mind get arrested in the pantry.

If you can construct, find, create a tunnel, that would be a great addition to the course and in that case you can begin to teach the puppy the word CRAWL. I would bait the length of the tunnel with tidbits for the first few trial runs and then eliminate the food gradually (one piece at a time) and reward the puppy with praise.

If you are building your obstacle course outdoors rather than setting up a movable course in your den or basement, and if your tiny puppy is going to grow up to be a Newfoundland or Irish Wolfhound, you will want to make the obstacle course huge enough so that, when teaching it or using it, you and your dog can go over, under, around and through as a duo. This kind of game, of course, is doubly wonderful if you have children. Watching them jump, crawl and cavort with your puppy will add much to your pleasure.

Have we, with all our fun and games, forgotten puppy's inspiring mother? No. Like her, we have kept his safety in mind every moment. Like her, we strive as we teach him to be clear, fair, loving. Like her, we observe with sensitivity, trying to know when to push forward and when to quit, when to praise softly in a nondisruptive fashion and when to correct obtrusively so that our puppy understands clearly what he should repeat and what he should forgo. And like her, we try to give the puppy a full range of experience—education, game playing, exercise, time to play with us, time to play and explore by himself and time to play and learn with his own kind.

Mother's perfect communication, her patience and understanding, her timing, her sureness, her kindness are all with us while we teach and play with our off-leash puppy.

7

Trouble Shooting

It takes two to tango.

SOMETIME BETWEEN your off-leash puppy work in a protected area and preparing for serious off-leash street work with your mature dog, you may find that your puppy/dog has some habits you'd like to change. He may bark a lot when you go out. He may *still* nip even though his weight is somewhere in the sixties now. He may even have been house-broken and then, for no particular reason, have started lifting his leg on the furniture! Or, your previous love-the-whole-world puppy may be growing up into a fearful, tail-tucking adult. You're in trouble. You need help.

We were all brought up to feel we could raise our children and dogs without help from anyone. But often, to our surprise and dismay, we cannot. Life is complicated and, in our time, the rules are changing so fast that it's hard to keep up with them. The things that used to be automatic a couple of generations back, aren't anymore. Many people need professional advice from books or experts in raising kids—and even in raising dogs. Modern man does not automatically take on the role of alpha dog and do everything properly. But this is not to say that if you have a dog problem it's your fault. Poor breeding practices have created a plethora of poor canine specimens and it is very possible that the dog you adore is shy or too aggressive because his parents were. At any rate, it doesn't help anyone for you to sit around blaming yourself if the dog urinates on the dining room table leg or hides when company comes. The thing to do is identify the problem, understand it and then fix it as best we can. Toward that end, this chapter will offer succinct help. However, if your dog problem is long-standing or quite complicated, or if you feel you need more details and advice, there is a clear, practical book on the subject that goes into this material in much more depth, devoting a chapter to each behavior problem. This book is called *Dog Problems* and I wrote it because these behavior problems were the inspiration for most of the calls I received as a professional trainer. It was clear to me that in our day and age, people did need help in raising and training dogs properly and I felt the call to take up arms against biting, destructiveness, shyness, car chasing, noise making and all the other problems that drove owners mad and sometimes sent dogs to the pound. That book is the ideal supplement to this chapter, which can only review the principles and methods for correcting and preventing behavior problems that often occur in growing and adult dogs. I'm proud of it and I recommend it highly to you.

Before going into specific problems your dog may be exhibiting, it would be both wise and helpful to review the possible reasons or combinations thereof why your dog is doing what he's doing. First, the choice of the parents who sired him may have been imprudent. Perhaps the breeder was inexperienced and didn't know better. But your dog may be nervous or shy, aggressive or intractable because of his genetic make-up. Next, he may have been in the kennel too long or too short. If he was kept too long by the breeder, he may not have been properly socialized. He may have never been off the breeder's property. In either case, he will exhibit some form of "kennelosis" or kennel shyness. This may be inspired by strangers, only men, only women, random people, children, one race or another or a walk off your property. In addition, your dog's problems may be caused by errors you made, not because you are a bad person or didn't care, but because you didn't know better. This last category will be the easiest to correct, but it may be the most difficult to understand. Here's why.

You already know that the dog is a pack animal and lives naturally in a loose family grouping that has one leader who calls the shots. Of course, if you have not taken on this role, using his mother as an example of fair, firm, loving stewardship, that lack in your dog's life will be the cause of his behavior problems. It is, in fact, one of the most common causes for acting up and acting out in dogs—and naturally, the reverse becomes the most ubiquitous, intelligent first step in correcting existing problems and preventing those not yet on the scene. But even beyond the dog's penchant to rise to power if you don't take a top dog role with him, there is another even more subtle reason why people get into so much trouble with dogs, a relationship planned and designed for mutual pleasure. It is because dogs are, as we've said, such accurate readers of nonverbal signals. If your lips say, "I'm in charge," but your body language does not, the dog will go by what really and truly is. The body does not lie. And his readings can be so fine tuned that you actually train your dog, unintentionally, by your reactions of pleasure and annoyance. These two emotions, in fact, are probably your very strongest training tools. Think about it—it's truly amazing to contemplate. The very subtle fact that you enjoy something your dog does will train him to do it again. And your feeling of displeasure or annoyance will be conveyed to him so clearly that it can be enough, by itself, to terminate other behavior. Here's how it works.

You are sitting at the coffee table having crackers and cheese with friends. Buddy approaches the table and stares at the food. He drools. "Isn't that cute?" you say. Buddy darts forward and ingests a hunk of gouda, about $3.85 worth to be exact. "Oh, Buddy, you're *such* a little thief," you say, giggling. "He loves gouda," you explain to your friends, excusing Buddy's behavior. Meanwhile, Buddy is planning the next siege on the coffee table. Buddy knows you think his stealing is cute. Maybe it's naughty, but it's soooo cute. Buddy is well on his way to becoming a hardened criminal. It's not only that you didn't correct Buddy. The real problem is that you actually enjoyed his daring, devil-may-care, free-spirited attitude. Perhaps, in your heart, you think a trained, well-behaved dog would be *dull*. Buddy knows what you think, don't you Buddy?

Even worse is the passive person who unconsciously is thrilled when his big dog growls at people in the street. (After all, who wants a sissy for a dog, right?) The average dog will know you want him to be a bully just as clearly as he knows you told him OK after he started to break a command. He'll escalate his untoward aggression until you've got a monster on your hands. "I tell him NO," you'll say. "But he won't listen." But Buddy *is* listening. He's attending to your body language. And he's listening to you soothe him by saying, "There, there, it's OK, good dog, calm down, there's a good boy," when he growls at an innocent person. Both your verbal and nonverbal messages are clear to your dog. *Aggression toward anyone who is near my master on the street is being positively reenforced. Therefore I am responsible to keep all comers away.*

Your puppy has a fine-tuned sensitivity. He will know if you think begging is amusing or aggression is thrilling or licking your hand is disgusting. Within the limits of his capabilities, he will respond and *get trained.*

It will be necessary, therefore, when you have a dog problem, to investigate all possible causes and use all possible resources, including your own feelings of pleasure and annoyance, to correct the behavior you do not want displayed. Instead of flinging blame, which does nothing to help the problem, you will seek the cause in order to better understand and be able to correct the problem. All problems can be ameliorated to some degree, though, sadly, some cannot be corrected enough to consider the dog as a good pet. Most loving owners will choose to live with a somewhat improved shy dog or a semireformed barker. But few will take anything less than perfection when it comes to serious problems of aggression. Now let's look at these difficulties one at a time.

ANXIETY

Dog owners rarely if ever think of anxiety as the cause of their dog problems, yet this unpleasant feeling is behind much of the bad behavior dogs exhibit and owners abhor. Just as it may well be the underlying cause in many human problems and just as we humans may find totally ineffective answers to our

own problems of anxiety, so the dog may indulge in destructive, ineffectual or even self-destructive habits when he is riddled with anxiety.

Why does the dog get anxious? First, because he is a pack animal and in our age and culture he is forced to spend much of his time alone. Being lonely makes him anxious and in his effort to relieve this misery, he may bark all day, tear up furniture, urinate randomly all over the house, whine and cry even after you get home, steal food, guard objects, make you miserable. In addition to his difficult adjustment to the loneliness of modern life, poor breeding practices make for dogs with exaggerated characteristics that cause problems: very shy, frightened dogs; over aggressive dogs; dogs who spend the day looking for imaginary enemies or standing guard over a stolen dish towel; psychopathic, unpredictable dogs; all other forms of genetic junk. Unwittingly and with the same Lassie fantasies anyone else has, you may have found a real mess to love.

Anxiety in dogs, which often leads to problem behavior, can also be caused by things you do—or don't do. First, if you are not pack leader to your dog, the lack of structure and authority in his life will make him anxious. Obedience training has a visible, immediate calming action on the dog. He knows who's boss. He knows the rules. He knows how to behave. Life is understandable, simple, sweet. Second, if his schedule is fairly regular, that will help allay anxiety. But if you are home at five one day and stay out until two in the morning the next without coming home to walk, feed and exercise your dog, he won't feel he knows what's going on and that feeling is one of anxiety. In order to relieve it, he'll chew, urinate, defecate, cry or whine.

Merely considering your dog's feelings is a giant step in relieving his anxious feelings and, therefore, in cutting down on behavior problems. Be his leader. Train him. Feed and walk him as regularly as you can. If your work life is so erratic that you can't be fair to a dog, you shouldn't have a dog. If you can't live without one, you'll simply have to hire a good-natured, dog-loving kid to come in and care for the dog when you cannot.

It helps, too, to give the dog a spot of his own—an old towel, a bed, a crate, a corner where he won't be bothered. And exercise is important. You know it helps *your* anxiety. It does the same for the dog. You might want to change your dog's diet. Some commercial dog foods are loaded with sugar and additives. A higher quality, plainer food will make your dog feel better. He doesn't need a constant supply of junk food, but a good, solid, plain diet fed at regular intervals.

Other tricks for helping the anxious dog are things like taking him out for a run around the block right before you leave, leaving a radio playing when you go out, saving a favorite chew toy for your absences and, if you want and can handle one, getting another pet for your pet, either a dog or a cat. But the most important step is the recognition that anxiety, not spite or stupidity, is the underlying cause of many behavior problems.

OWNER FEAR

Please, even if you feel completely comfortable with your dog, read this section. Sooner or later, probably sooner, you will see this common syndrome in a friend and this brief section might enable you to help both the friend and his dog. As long as we have discussed dog anxiety, we must, in all fairness, discuss owner anxiety or fear of dogs.

Surprisingly, quite a few people buy dogs even though they are afraid of them. Some, at least, buy little dogs. Others go plunging ahead and buy the very type of dog they fear most—a Shepherd, Doberman or Rottweiler. In either case, the presence of the dog usually makes the fear worse. This is so because fear of dogs is often unconscious and so the person is not dealing directly with it. However, the dog knows it's there. This prevents the owner from becoming top dog. The top dog would never be afraid of underlings. Of course, without leadership, training tends to go astray. Now the dog, untrained and leaderless, will tend to act out in very destructive, dominating ways. If he is large and assertive, he will become dangerous to the owner and anyone else who happens to get in his way. This then fulfills and reenforces the owner's deepest fears.

While I have helped people to see this problem in themselves and have helped some owners overcome their fears, I strongly doubt that people with this particular problem can get

out of it without outside help. A book or a class may be help enough. But for some, only sessions with a private trainer will do. Here they can learn to understand both the dog and themselves, learn to read the signs and signals the dog is giving them, learn to handle and control the dog, tighten the training, take charge and eventually enjoy the dog and have an appropriate relationship with it.

Some owners, though, no matter how sensitively the subject is introduced, will not accept the fact that they are afraid. I worked with a young couple once who had inherited a Doberman. I make this point because the dog was of excellent breeding and no responsible breeder would have sold a large, male Doberman to this very passive couple. I met the wife first and she owned up to her problem, though it took me quite a while to show her how strongly it affected the dog. She had trouble seeing that he was not only a good animal, but a great one and that his bad behavior was caused by her fear and her lack of assertion with him. My only chance was the husband, but when I met him, all hope died. He flatly refused to consider the fact that he was afraid of the dog. At one point, just as he was telling me that he wasn't the least bit afraid, the dog barked at another dog in the distance. The young man flinched and then blinked nervously for several awkward, painful moments. He was terrified. Unable to get through to him about his fear, I began to try to explain what an awful mistake it was for him to keep an animal of that size that he couldn't, for whatever reason, control. Among other things, I asked my child to take the leash and the dog happily obeyed her without hesitation. She had complete, easy control. But they still refused to see that the dog was intractible because of their underlying fear of him. One day, after many difficult lessons, they broke an appointment with me and simply disappeared. I cannot imagine that the story had a very happy ending.

Owner fear can be overcome, but it must first be seen by the fearful person. You cannot get over something you won't own up to having in the first place. Sometimes a person will realize that they are uncomfortable around the particular dog they have chosen, but they feel okay with small dogs. In this case, the trainer can help the person place the dog with another family and help the owner find a smaller, less dominant dog to love.

If you should feel, reading this, that you might have a pocket of fear, perhaps from a childhood bite or frightening incident, your best bet is to join a training class or hire a private, professional trainer. After all, when you have control of your dog, when you can play with him and enjoy him but still be in charge, when you understand what makes him tick, he must become less an object of fear, even unconscious fear, and more the friend you desired when you chose him. In this case, the work and effort and time and money will give you the double gift of true companionship from your dog and the satisfaction of overcoming an uncomfortable, hidden feeling. I have, I am happy to say, seen people become understanding, assertive and virtually fearless with dogs that previously were ruling the household. It's a turnabout that *always* makes master, dog and trainer feel terrific.

SHYNESS

Shyness is an epidemic problem among dogs. Much of this comes from poor breeding practices and from poor socialization. That is, many dogs are bred despite problems of shyness. In addition, many puppies of shy or sound breeding are not properly exposed to a variety of human beings and experiences when they are young. Some are also kept in the kennel too long. If a dog is bred from spooky stock and/or doesn't have the chance to overcome fear of change when he is young, he will grow up shy and fearful.

You can help a shy dog by gradually exposing him to new people and places and by praising him for holding his ground in new situations. Training is essential. By making the shy dog heel, you prevent him from hiding behind you or trying to run away everytime a kid comes running down your street. Eventually, you should have strangers handle him. The easiest way to do that is to put the dog on a sit stay and make him do it. In addition and most important of all, never comfort the shy dog with petting and soothing words when he is shaking, tucking his tail,

Benjamin

trying to escape. To the dog, your petting and soothing will be understood as praise for spooky behavior and you will actually be training your dog to be more shy. Instead, praise him for acting bold, for holding his ground, for staying when you make some noise, for letting a child pet him gently, for walking on a new block, for going into stores, etc. Shyness is responsive to training and I have seen many shy dogs gradually become more outgoing with careful, sensitive owner handling.

No matter how outgoing your shy dog becomes, you should not breed it. There's too great a chance the shy personality would be passed on to the puppies. There are far too many shy dogs around already.

You may disagree with me, thinking that your shy dog is still a pretty nice pet. So what if she doesn't love everyone in sight. Who cares? But even if you like your shy dog exactly the way she is, she doesn't like herself that way. Shyness hurts. The shy dog suffers the same kind of pangs the shy person feels. No one should knowingly wish that kind of pain on any creature.

Sometimes the shy dog, a disappointment to its owners, will be put on a back burner, neglected because it isn't outgoing and fun. This makes the shy dog more shy. Don't leave your fearful dog at home to spend his day confronting his own fears. Get him out and around. The more he realizes he won't die from meeting strangers, the less shy he'll eventually feel.

AGGRESSION

How can one be brief about aggression? This is the most difficult area of dog training. Even with good advice, if your dog is biting, you probably will have to hire a dog trainer. Though some dogs seem to be just waiting for an alpha dog to show up on the scene, and these bad apples reform very quickly when given a set of rules to live by, other dogs just won't quit. You start to correct their terrible ways and they escalate. It takes a lot of nerve to work with a biting dog. And it takes a lot of heart and courage to know when it's too late to save the dog, too.

If your dog is well bred, well trained, well fed, exercised, loved, groomed, played with and understood, you should not have to read this section. You have already dealt with nipping

172

SUBMISSIVE

IN TRANSITION

DOMINANT!

and with normal adolescent testing. A biting problem should not just crop up from nowhere if a healthy dog is being well raised. However, it may seem that that is just precisely what is happening.

Possibly you have missed your dog's testing, his quiet, even passive looking escalation. You may have made excuses (He's just a dog. He'll outgrow it. Don't all dogs do that?). You have, perhaps unconsciously, begun to mold your life around your dog's growing aggression.

On the other hand, your dog may have developed a health problem that is connected to his aggression. Perhaps he's got hip dysplasia or his coat is so badly matted underneath that it pulls at his skin and he bites when he's in pain. It might be a case of, "If I hurt and you're standing there, it must be your fault." Maybe he's got a tumor—or he's simply gone mad. Humans have these tragic problems. So do dogs.

Most likely, you've missed a few important messages as you were raising Buddy. (After all, you're not his mother. You're not even of his species.) In this case, your dog's aggression did not just crop up out of nowhere. It rarely does. He has been testing you to see if he could apply for alpha dog—and you've been consistently failing his tests. You're not a bad person. You're busy, distracted, and you didn't understand. At the same time, chances are you gave him some messages that let him know he could take charge. Of course, you didn't mean to do that. But when he growled at the postman you always comforted him, inadvertently praising him for inappropriate aggression. He got the message—and so did the postman. Now your mail is on the sidewalk instead of the porch. And little by little your dog got the idea that there was no one is the driver's seat, so, being a dog, he simply slid over. Now you've got to set him straight.

If you are in this kind of trouble, one of the things you'll have to do is to stop ignoring your gut feelings. You already know when your dog is getting pushy, is escalating, is looking for trouble. Act on these feelings. Snap on the lead. Take him out for a lesson. If he's looking nuts, crate him until he cools off. When your stomach tells you he's going to bite, don't let your head make excuses.

Once I saw that all-important glassy look in a dog's eyes and I took a bite on purpose. It was too late to stop the dog, but not too late to grab the leash from the owner. She was a little old lady who had rescued the dog from the pound. I knew if he bit her, he'd go right back there, and fast. I took the leash and the bite so that I could get a chance to correct the dog immediately after the fact, which I did. I also hoped that if I made light of my wound, she'd give the dog another chance. Oddly, it's the only bite I ever got that left a scar, a tiny white ridge near my left thumb. The bite was only a scratch, an impotent bid for leadership from a nervous, confused little mutt. Unfortunately, my master plan did not work. The lady and her dog never returned to class.

Why do I relate such an unflattering story—a failure? Because once a grown dog is biting, many honest efforts at rehabilitation will end in failure. In addition, many efforts to save a biter will get you bitten. If these two facts seem unappealing, by all means hire a good dog trainer to help you straighten out your dog—or, if you know it's too late for all that, put the dog to sleep.

With or without a professional trainer, here's an outline of what you have to do to reform an adult biting dog:

1. Tighten all obedience work so that the dog does what he is told, where he is told, when he is told and for as long as he is told, no excuses! All this must hold true in the face of distractions such as children playing, normal household routine, other animals moving around, guests visiting, noise other than his own.

2. Increase the amount of exercise the dog receives. You should make a strong effort to use up as much as possible of the dog's energy in constructive exercise. This may include the hour or more you practice obedience work with him as well as jogging, swimming, chasing a ball, whatever you can safely get him to do.

3. Reward the dog with attention only when he has just behaved well. Doting on an animal gives him the message that he is top dog. It is only the top dog who is doted on in a pack. If your dog is biting, he knows he's top dog. In order

to change his mind, in addition to the other items on this list, stop doting on him. In fact, when he solicits attention, ignore him. Do not allow him to bully you into petting or play sessions. Stop and think about why you are petting him and begin to do so for the execution of commands and not because his majesty demands it.

4. Correct all signs of aggression. Discontinue making any excuses for growling, nipping, bullying, biting, territorial marking in inappropriate places, object guarding, bratty behavior.

5. Keep correctional aids handy so that you will be able to correct your dog without getting bitten. These include lemon juice to squirt in his snarling face, collar and leash, crate, pot of water to dump on his head if need be. If one of your problems of aggression is dog fighting, your two best tools are a leash for prevention and lemon juice for stopping a fight in progress. If there are loose aggressive dogs where you walk your dog, carry the lemon juice along on his walks.

6. Be clear in your corrections. Work like his mother. Shake him by the collar, using the leash as added protection if the dog is really aggressive. Then confine the dog for one hour. If the dog tries to bite you, use a squirt of lemon juice in his mouth to make him back off. If you are afraid of the dog, hire professional help to correct the dog and to help you build back your confidence with him.

7. Set a time limit. If you are working on your own, set a limit of, say, about three weeks. If, at the end of that time, there is no visible improvement, either hire a trainer or put the dog to sleep. It is neither wise nor safe to go on and on with a biter if he is not improving.

Some trainers (choose yours carefully) making sweeping promises about stopping aggression. But in this tough area, even written guarantees do not make for cured dogs. Once an adult dog has bitten several times, the prognosis must be guarded. Indeed, hard work may bring him around. But he will never be as reliable as the dog who has never bitten anyone. There must always be some caution in dealing with a biter, even a reformed one. Be warned. Prevention is most appealing when it comes to aggression. And miracles, while so seductive, rarely happen in the real world.

Of course give the dog every reasonable chance, following the above guidelines. But if he ends up worse or the same, do not give him away. Have him destroyed. Then cry your heart out without shame. Even the biggest hooligan is loved by his mother—and, in this case, by his owner as well.

CHRONIC HOUSEBREAKING PROBLEMS

The dog over six months old who is still having accidents is a problem. By now, your patience is justifiably thin. Unless the dog is having accidents because he is ill or neglected, you should come down hard on him and get the job of housebreaking over and done with. This includes the dog who is busy marking his territory off within your lovely home.

You must buy and use a crate. There is no choice unless you want your dog to remain unhousebroken forever. Put the dog on a schedule, just as if you had a tiny puppy, and crate him in between walks. For the first week, treat him exactly as if he were a puppy, keeping him in the crate much of the time. That will get his attention! Then begin to keep him out when you know he'll be good. Watch him like a hawk. Crate him when you are not home. Make sure he does what he's supposed to do on his walks and praise him for doing so. If a walk is a dud, put him right into the crate until the next walk.

You do not have to have an unhousebroken dog. By using the crate, a schedule, the eyes of an eagle, you can housebreak *any* dog, even a Beagle! Keep vigilant. Keep clean. Keep using the crate until the job is done. When you're sure it is, invite me to tea—but *please*, not before! Get the point?

BARKING, WHINING, CRYING

There are three things you can do with a noisy dog. First, you can do nothing. In this case, the dog will keep barking whenever he feels like it and you may end up enemies with your neighbors, evicted or a victim of chronic headaches. Second, you

can correct the dog whenever he goes on his noise-making marathons. You can even pretend to leave and sneak back to the house. Then, when the concert begins, you can break in on him, yelling NO, NO, NO, NO, shake him by the collar and make him wish, at least for the moment, that he was never born. The third possibility, the Serendipitous Method described in *Dog Problems*, is that you can teach the dog to do what he's doing on command, thereby gaining control of the activity. Since when you issue a command, the dog focuses on you, you will readily be able to stop what you have started. Thus the dog who speaks on command shuts up on command as well. SPEAK is what turns him on. ENOUGH will turn him off. And amen to that!

There's a fourth choice when it comes to noisy dogs because some of the noise they make isn't really conscious. This is particularly true when it comes to whining. How can you correct something the dog doesn't even know he's doing? Easy! Do it with him. Imitation is not only a form of flattery. It's a form of dog training. Cry and whine along with your dog and soon enough, the second or third concert, he'll begin to show the light of recognition in his eyes. In fact, he'll love the idea of doing duets with you.

I hear you. You're saying, "Who cares?" You're saying, "Just make him shut up." Aren't you?

Think MOM. Patience will be rewarded. Once your dog looks at you and whines with you, you can add a word to your madness, the word SPEAK. Now, after your dog will SPEAK on command, with and without you, begin to intrude on this activity—whether you have started it or not—with the magic word ENOUGH. If your dog continues to sing, grasp the collar, say ENOUGH once more and shake, adding harsh eye contact to your correction.

Of course, you may have unintentionally trained your dog to whine, cry and bark by reenforcing this annoying behavior. To find out, make a checklist of what makes your dog whine and bark and how you respond when he does:

1. Buddy barks. I give him a cookie to quiet him.
2. Buddy barks when I'm on the phone. I lean over and pet him to quiet him.

3. Buddy whines when my spouse and I make love. We let him up on the bed to quiet him.

Uh oh! Guess who's in trouble! Follow methods above, teaching your dog to bark on command and then stopping him with ENOUGH, harsh eye contact and a shake. Never give your dog anything, including the time of day, when he's barking, whining or crying for it. Use the long down once a day, tighten up your training and make sure the dog is quiet before you feed him, walk him, pet him. If the dog bothers you while you are watching TV, reading, dining or making love, squirt him in the mouth with lemon juice and go on about your business.

Noise making may seem a lesser crime than biting or destructiveness, but it can have serious consequences. In fact, it may be a sign of escalation. To stop that, as well as for its pure annoyance, it should be put under control as soon as possible.

DESTRUCTIVENESS

A lot of people get disgusted with their dogs, even give up on them permanently, because of destructive behavior, such as chewing, digging, shredding, scratching doors. Some people who have their dogs killed by the local vet or the humane society—let's not use euphemisms here—think a crate is cruel. Let's get something clear right now. Which do you think is more cruel, the use of a dog crate as a temporary training tool or death?

If you raise your dog with a crate, you will never have to worry about coming home to find a shredded couch. When you cannot watch the dog, crate him. As he matures and excels in training, as he proves himself capable of being left loose in your home, give him the privileges he so richly deserves. Do not give him responsibility he cannot handle. That would be like giving a four-year-old your car keys!

Beside the crate, understanding is an important tool in stopping destructive behavior. Dogs chew for a variety of reasons and these must be reviewed along with companion remedies. Your dog will chew to release pent up energy. Make sure he gets enough exercise. Your dog will chew because he is

anxious. He may be left alone too long and too often. Give him a little more consideration when making plans. Train him so that you can take him with you more often. Train him to allay his anxiety, his feeling of looseness and lack of connection. Hire a nice kid to come and walk him when you are out to work. Think of what a little job like that would have meant to you when you were a little kid and would have stood on your nose for a dollar. Think, too, of what it will mean to your dog.

Dogs chew when they are bored. Leave your dog something acceptable to chew. In that way, he'll be less likely to chew what's yours. Dogs chew because they don't know they are not supposed to. Are you clear when you correct your dog? Do you give him socks to play with and then get mad when he chews your clothes? Bitches shred just before coming into heat. Keep your female's cycle on a calendar and watch for signs that she is coming into heat: increased appetite, increased displays of affection, increased activity level, generally hyper behavior. You may have to crate her just before the onset of her heat cycle—or, if not, at least provide her with a supply of shred-dables to practice her nest making on. So, here's the formula: Use a crate when necessary. Your dog should be reliable sometime between one and two years of age. Exercise your dog. Leave your dog some rawhide or other safe chew toys. Monitor his behavior when you are with him, correcting him with a NO for starting to work on the fringe of the carpet or the arm of the sofa. Then present him with one of his toys and tell him OK. But if he goes right back to your stuff, correct him again and put him in the crate for one hour. Tighten your obedience work. This reenforces you as top dog, someone not to be trifled with. And, if you are gone long hours, hire a nice neighborhood kid to come and walk your dog and play with him.

Now, what about hole digging in the yard? Here's my solution: I side with the puppy's mother. I know that digging is both natural and pleasurable for dogs. So I let my dog have her pleasure. I divide the yard, giving a corner to my dog in which she may dig to her heart's delight. I fence the corner, making it a pen or run. Once a week, I hire a nice kid to fill in the holes and tamp them down. When the dog is in my part of the yard, I

Dogs chew when they are bored.

Correct him with a NO!

I let my dog have her pleasure.

184

correct her if she tries to dig up the lawn, eat azaleas (they're poisonous anyway) or dash through the flower beds. That means that when I am not out, the dog is not in the fancy part of the yard. It's a good compromise. I recommend it.

RUNNING AWAY

When I do radio call-in shows, lots of the questions have to do with running away. The natural solution, or so I'm told, is to property train the dog, teaching him to stay within the boundaries of your property as if he were a surveyor and not a dog at all. That's what I call the easy life. I also call it a fantasy.

I'd like to go on record here and now on property training. Mother knows best. The dog is a roaming animal. The notion of property training is foreign to him, against his very nature. Therefore, you can property train him—but it won't really work. He may dash to the end of your lawn or land and not put a toe onto the road. You can tempt him with treats, another dog, clapping and hooting. No. He won't come. Not your dog. I've seen it. Then, a week, month or even a year later, the right temptation comes along, a jogger with a juicy looking calf or a succulent-looking squirrel or the scent of a dog in heat and your property training is gone. And when he goes, my friend, that might be just when a truck is barreling down your road. Don't take chances. Please.

If you don't want your dog to run away, use a leash. Train him and go out with him off leash so that you can stop him with a verbal command. Install an overhead run and hook him up to that when he's out alone. But don't count on him to go against his nature and perform the impossible. He's just a dog. One day he'll forget and that day could be his last.

JUMPING UP

I confess. At the time of this writing, my dog, Scarlet, still jumps up on people. After scrupulously training hundreds of dogs never to do it, something in me needed the exuberant, all out, *painful* hello that Scarlet delivers. But at long last I have come to my senses and I am now in the process of teaching her

186

not to throw her seventy or so pounds at me or my friends when she wants to say hello. There are lots of good reasons to teach your dog not to jump up and practically no reason to let her do it. Any dog can learn to deliver tons of affection from the floor and to forgo scaring people, knocking over little kids, tearing and messing up clothing, acting like an hysterical jerk just because you brought in the mail.

First, do not make a production of coming and going. When you come home, greet your dog warmly, but casually. Immediately ask him to sit. Next, holding onto his collar to prevent a sudden loss of teeth from an unexpected jump, pet the dog, without hysterical baby talk, while he is seated. Then go about your business.

When your dog jumps up on you, slip your hand into his collar and pull him harshly off to the side, firmly placing his feet back on the ground. Praise immediately. When you see your dog getting ready to fly at someone else, tell him NO JUMPING, SIT, GOOD BOY. If that is not enough to stop him, leash him. As he begins the jump, jerk back hard saying NO JUMPING, SIT, GOOD DOG. The job will take about a month if you are *consistent* and will not get done at all if you give in and let the dog jump up to kiss you when you are in the mood and not wearing silk. Did you hear that, Benjamin?!!

If it's any comfort, I'll be working with my dog while you work with yours. So, who's perfect?

THE RING-WISE DOG

Those who compete in obedience are fond of, and overuse, the phrase, "a ring-wise dog." This is the dog who works perfectly in class—when he can be corrected if he goofs—and refuses to retrieve, jump or come when in the obedience ring where the rules clearly state that no corrections may be made. There is no such thing as a ring-wise dog, my friends, only an owner-wise dog.

If your dog clearly shows you, in your yard or in class, that he understands any given command or signal and then he categorically refuses to do it in the ring, then there is something wrong with the basic dog/owner relationship. The term "ring-

188

wise" would indicate that the dog, knowing he cannot be corrected in the ring, spitefully refuses the proferred work for the purpose of hurting, humiliating and dumping anger on his owner. Now, why would a dog act this way?

Perhaps you have lost the balance in your relationship, thinking more of high scores than you do of your friendship with your dog. You might even purchase dogs or choose breeds that tend to score high in the ring, placing this potential above all other aspects of the relationship. Maybe when you aren't involved in formal training, your dog is in a kennel or a crate. Does he like this? NO. Does he know how you feel about him and about obedience work? YES. Is he ring-wise? Sure he is. But, more important, he's owner-wise. He's delivering a message, perhaps in the only way he can get it through to you. Heed it. It's eloquent.

Years ago I was asked to prepare a famous show dog for the obedience ring. His owner was very busy with his business, his younger dogs, his family and his friends and didn't have time to get Leo ready for a CD, that which stood between the dog and a Register of Merit listing. I thought Leo was the cat's pajamas. I was thrilled to be able to work with him and I lavished attention on him the likes of which made us great friends. I invented games for Leo, I groomed him after his lessons, I sang songs to him, I gazed admiringly at him, I took him home and let him sleep on my bed.

In no time, this brilliant, polished, seasoned, beautiful animal learned the CD work and did it for me with near perfection. But when his owner whipped him into the car and took him to a dog show, Leo not only didn't get the desired leg, he walked out of the ring.

Leo was not getting the attention he had gotten as a young show prospect, the attention he had been trained to need. Without getting, he wasn't giving. He wasn't ring-wise. He was miserable. He only wanted what every dog wants—love and attention. Without that, Leo didn't have much to give.

If you have a ring-wise dog, stop working for the ring and the degree for at least six weeks. Instead, play with your dog, enjoy his company, forget about being judged and scored, but try to see the separate individual who has been leading you off the path to glory. For at least a while, go for laughs and mutual understanding. When you resume your competition practice, pay your dog for his time. His salary will be interesting lessons. Don't drone on and on for a perfect sit. Who's perfect? And reward your Leo after the session with a run, a romp, a game he can win, a ride in the car to the lake for a swim. Put the balance back in your dog/person relationship. If you want to get, you've got to give.

And now, a final thought on dealing with dog problems—

DISCIPLINE IS NOT A FOUR-LETTER WORD

Discipline should be as much a part of the normal life of a pack animal as are companionship, play, cooperation and affection. In the wild, the alpha dog will give daily reminders of his lofty position. He does this not because there is discord in the family. He does it to prevent the notion of conflict, rivalry, mutiny. Thus, he requires the members of his pack to live by the rules—his. He instills in them, by his reminders, a sense of self-discipline. There are regulations by which the others must abide. When they do, they are loved, they are safe, peace reigns.

Under the benevolent, masterful eye of an intelligent, strong leader, the dogs are as stress-free as possible. Life has order and calm. Within these bounds there is room and time for play, for humor, for love. It's simply a case of spare the rod and spoil the pack.

Under the umbrella of discipline, human pack leaders must face a variety of choices. Easiest, perhaps, is selecting to be pack leader. At least for those dog owners who clearly understand the nature of the dog as a pack animal, there is no other sensible choice. In theory, this is acceptable, even to very sentimental owners with anthropomorphic views of their dogs. But in practice, leadership is more difficult than it sounds. The wolf or dog in a wild setting has an instinctual barometer that guides him in correcting his own. Not being of the same species is a great disadvantage when it comes to discipline. The big question then is: Just how do we remind our dogs—gently, effectively,

humanely, clearly—that we are in charge? When is our "discipline" too soft, too little, ineffective? When do we rule with an iron hand? How can we tell if we are too weak or too rough? Do we remind as humans or as dogs? How do we deal with this closet topic in a world that still thinks discipline is a dirty word?

Nonviolent Assertiveness

The easiest way to remind our dogs of that all-important message is via the use of obedience training. The training itself establishes your social dominance over the dog. Then the commands can be used as appropriate, authentic reminders of your relative positions. Does the animal mind being reminded that you are up and he is down? Indeed not. Even the most assertive dog feels the sense of calm that comes from clear leadership. Remember, it's lonely at the top. By taking charge, you are lifting from the shoulders of your pet the burdens of decision making, protection, leadership. He is free to enjoy his well-structured life with little anxiety. He only has to worry about pleasing you. And you are quite easy to please, no?

The long down, a sit stay, a good session of heeling, all these activities are double duty with the dog. They give you the control over his behavior you might need at the moment. At the same time they remind the dog, in a most gentlemanly way, that you are in charge. Most dogs will be visibly calmer after a training session than when they are in the middle of testing you, attempting to steal the scepter of power. That struggle causes conflict for the dog. Your assertiveness removes the conflict. Thus, daily "discipline" is the kindest gift you can give your animals.

But what happens when the testing gets tough? What happens when the dog wonders, "What will the bimbo do if I don't obey his lousy commands?" When adolescence strikes and your dog vies with you for leadership—or any time after that when Buddy decides to see what he's made of—how then do we "remind" in a way that is sane, appropriate, effective? When corrections come into the discipline picture, opinions tend toward extremes. In a room full of dog experts, no two might agree on just the sort and dose required by the behavior of the moment.

192

The long down reminds Buddy that you are in charge.

Getting Physical

Let's return to the pack in the wild for a moment. Here we can see that there is a variety of methodology for maintaining leadership of a group of canids. First, there is the assertive stare—what my high school students used to call "the eye." It works. And it can work for you as well as for a wolf. In fact, one of the most urgent matters of dog raising should be that of teaching the dog to make eye contact with you, to actually look to you for approval and disapproval. Practicing this with young dogs will condition the dog to behave in this way. And it is indeed thrilling to be out with your dog and when a question arises concerning his behavior, have him look into your eyes for the answer. You will find your dog's eyes eloquent beyond belief, and that your own ability to send messages from and to the eyes increases as you relate in this deep and quiet way. Naturally, all your eye contact with your dog will not be harsh and assertive. Most will be soft and loving. But if he is in the habit of looking to you, you will be in the position to veto behavior with your eyes alone.

The wild ones use sounds, too, to "remind." So can you. You need not growl to be effective. In fact, a clearing of the throat can remind your dog to look into your eyes—and a gasping inhale is one of the strongest corrections I've seen with a dog who knows your position. The gasp translates, "How dare you?"

So far, we are on pretty safe ground. But we are fast leaving it for a stroll on thin ice. Back with the pack, corrections escalate to the physical now. The leader may grasp the muzzle of the offender and just hold it or use his hold to flip the other to his back. The body language with which the weaker answers is that mechanism that stops the "attack" so that the reminder, although violent looking, remains pretty peaceable. If you and your dog are in conflict and someone is getting hurt, think about the pack. Something has gone amiss and you, as leader, have the responsibility to right it.

When your dog requires a stronger correction than harsh eye contact or a verbal correction (either a sound or a word or words, NO, BAD DOG, NO BITING, etc.), you will have the

The assertive stare works!

problem of carefully judging the nature of the correction and the amount. I cannot do that for you. This topic, then, is among the most difficult to address because the decision of what to do, when to do it and how strongly to come on is often a combination of knowledge plus gut feeling and comes from what you know about and sense in the dog in question. The written word cannot replace the personal contact required to tell you when to laugh off your dog's brattiness (seriously) and when to grab his collar, lift him slightly and "fly" him into a down stay. There are, however, some guidelines we can discuss.

First of all, physical correction is a natural consequence of being a dog. It is, therefore, something that can be fair and can be understood. Withholding dinner as a punishment for a housebreaking accident is out of the vocabulary of your dog and therefore something he cannot understand. This does not mean you can only act like a dog in correcting Buddy. While the collar shake is imitative of bitch-to-pup corrections, a leash correction seems to be in the ballpark, too. That is, it works. It appears to be humane and the dog appears to understand it.

Perhaps the most difficult part of discipline is understanding (as implied earlier) when the dog is genuine and when the dog is trying to pull your leg. Again, it is the in-person experience that reveals the bully and the goldbricker. However, knowing that both are possible helps you to make the decision. Once the computer (you) has the information, it is usually processed in seconds. Then you must correct, trying to remain within your dog's body language, and you must assess the results. Not being naturals (that is, the same species) at this kind of communication (and discipline is communication if it is to be effective), we must try things, saving some and rejecting others. If you have given your all to your rotten dog and he misbehaves again immediately, either you were not clear or you were too weak in your correction. If your dog falls apart when you jerk the leash, shove him angrily into a down stay or shake him by the collar, then either you have overcorrected and used too much force or your dog is the best actor in the world. Of course, both are possible.

Usually we handle our dogs in the same style in which we do

The collar shake is imitative of bitch-to-pup corrections.

everything else. That is, the assertive, even rough, person will come on strong with his dog. In his case (or hers), thought should be given to more nonphysical communication and discipline. An effort should be made to tone down the roughness in fairness to the dog. The very mild person, the one who makes the longest list of excuses before correcting anything, should try to excuse less and get more physical with the dog. This may mean using the shake for large transgressions and good, strong leash corrections for errant behavior. Both extremes should, understanding their own characters, try in dog rearing to come closer to the middle ground.

There is no substitute for knowing your dog. Without that, matters of discipline can only be guess work. Beyond that, we must remind ourselves, perhaps daily, of the need to remind our dogs that their lives are filled not only with love and fun, but with structure and leadership as well. Discipline is not a four-letter word. It is the basis of community life, that which we humans share with our pack friends, the dogs. With consistency and thoughtfulness we can offer our dogs the best mixed-species pack life possible.

Their lives are filled not only with love and fun, but with structure and leadership as well.

8
Class

*My own criteria of success is the ability
to work joyfully and to live positively.*

A. S. Neill
Summerhill

WHEN I MOVED to the upper, upper West side of Manhattan, to the neighborhood around Columbia University, and began to take my German Shepherd puppy to the park for exercise and play, I found an interesting group of my neighbors, there for the same purpose. The group of dogs was very mixed, some having been abandoned on the street or in the park and rescued, some having been adopted from local animal shelters, some of less humble origins, some purebreds—one of which was even a champion. This odd social set met daily while their proud owners kept a careful vigil. First, we made sure all the dogs played within our sight. Second, we watched out for volatile behavior and possible fights, however, with space, freedom and daily socialization, scraps rarely occurred. Third, our eyes were sharp (our plastic bags ready) so that we could obey the scoop law. Last, but, oh, not least, we were all on the alert for the van, the infamous vehicle that transported the park rangers and their books of tickets. Letting dogs off leash to exercise and play is against the law in New York City. None of us was a stranger to the stiff fifty dollar fine. Indeed, this particular law had been the subject of many angry discussions. While we all understood the reasons for the law, we were angered that there were no exceptions, places in the park or hours when it would be legal to exercise our dogs. In addition, it was clear that the law was capriciously enforced, ticketing being more severe on the West side than the East. However, antidog sentiment being strong in Manhattan, we felt we had no chance at all in making legal changes. All we could do was scoop and continue to peer through the bushes for a glimpse of the van, paranoid to a man. I was filled with admiration for this devoted group of responsible dog owners. That's when the idea for forming a dog class began.

A DOG CLASS FOR ALL SEASONS

Since we all intended to continue giving our dogs the good life, we decided we needed more than basic training (which most of the dogs didn't have anyway). What this group needed was basic training plus a dazzling off-leash recall—a fifty dollar come when called! Having "retired" from dog training to write full time and missing the hands-on work with dogs, I eagerly agreed to find a space and teach a dog class right in the neighborhood.

After some initial procrastination and a frustrating, unsuccessful search for indoor space, I got the idea that I should *truly* fill the need of this neighborhood. I decided to teach the dogs in the very environment in which they had to obey the commands—and fast—right in Riverside Park. It was a challenge, to be sure, to take a mixed group of dogs (as it turned out, the age range in class was four-and-a-half months to seven years) and work them outdoors where accoustics were poor, the weather was unpredictable and other loose dogs were playing. Perhaps it was that very challenge that propelled me into action and so early in October of that year, I dropped all else one day and worked out the mechanics for my new project—dog school in the park, a dog class for all seasons.

The first problem was publicity. I couldn't teach a class if I didn't have students. Even though I had a core group of enthusiastic owners, I understood that enthusiasm is often higher for a notion than it is for a reality. I decided it would be better to let the other dog owners in the neighborhood in on our idea.

It seemed to me that the less the class cost, the more it would suit this neighborhood, an area of highly educated, careful spenders. So I decided against advertising and in favor of a hand delivered flyer. I made up a flyer, had it xeroxed, folded it for easier carrying and prepared for my daily run with my then eleven-month-old Shepherd. I chose "the rush hour" rather than taking a solitary noon time run so that I would see the majority of dog owners out with their dogs. As we jogged, I simply handed flyers to people with dogs, saying breathlessly in passing, "We're starting a dog class Saturday. Hope you can come." The flyer explained where to meet and when, and what would be taught in class. It also stated that the class was "pay as you go," at the rate of ten dollars per class.

About thirty-five people promised to come, applauding the idea of a dog class right in the park. On the morning of the first class, I had knots in my stomach. I didn't know if I'd be swamped with students and have to divide the class in thirds or if I'd show up at "the big rock" where we were to meet and find myself alone with my Shepherd and the trees. Something told me it would be the latter. However, by 10:30, a half an hour after class was scheduled to begin, I had five students ready to work. Since Scarlet worked in class, too, first with me and later with my husband as handler, we began with six dogs, a nice, intimate group.

I started class with the sit stay to propel our students into the right mental framework for training. Although it is traditional to begin with heeling, I feel that it is very important to get the attention of the dogs first by teaching a sit and stay and by pushing just a little on the stay. Very quickly even dogs with no training at all learn that the master means business and how the leash works to enforce training. This done, we moved rapidly into the heel. This was excellent because all the dogs must be walked on leash much of the time and the work uses up some of the boundless energy the dogs bring to class.

Not counting the one- or two-time students (a retriever-type from the local shelter, a Corgi with a CD, a young Springer

Spaniel), we had a fine, loyal core group of four dogs. Jamie was the oldest dog, a seven-year-old male with a passion for retrieving sticks and balls. He had been "an unsolicited birthday present" to Scott, a postdoctoral chemist at Columbia. Jamie was untrained and "only listened when he felt like it." But he had other problems, too. He had been taken from his litter too young and as a result was not sociable with other dogs. I told Scott that I had seen very satisfactory results in obedience training older dogs, but that the loss of early socialization could never be made up. I didn't think Jamie would ever get more friendly to other dogs. Benson was also adopted from a shelter, but Benson was a social butterfly. He was friendly to humans and dogs, soft and easygoing in manner, very amenable to obedience work. His coowners, Richard and Polly, both work with children at New York Hospital. They not only wanted to do everything right with and for Ben, they were hoping one day to take him into the hospital to cheer up the children. This was one of the ideas that took fire as the group got acquainted and got hooked on dog work. We decided to prepare the whole group of four dogs to "entertain" in children's wards and nursing homes, to show off what we had taught our dogs and also to give back something valuable to the community in which we lived. Richard, by the way, was the only owner from the original dog play group who came to dog class and stayed.

Ernie was the baby of the class and the only nonneighborhood dog to attend. He and his writer owner Bruce walked four miles each way from their East side apartment to join us. Ernie is a Sussex Spaniel, one of the rarest breeds in the United States today and Bruce had waited for over two years to get him. Ernie got a lot of attention, of course, because no one had ever seen a Sussex before. Sometimes people passing would even interrupt class to ask what kind of dog Ernie was. My only concern for Ernie was his age. Dogs under six months old working with older dogs can feel the strain. So for the first two classes, Ernie got a couple of extra rest and play breaks. After this, he was well able to keep up with the older dogs. This was so because he is a very strong, healthy pup and also because the class was small and outdoors. Furthermore, play breaks were a regular part of

Your dog will enjoy working with other working dogs.

Ernie was the baby of the class.

Any number can work—

or play.

our curriculum, so none of the dogs showed any signs of stress. The fourth dog was the only bitch in class, my own indulged German Shepherd, Scarlet, who turned one year old the day school began. Scarlet already did a dazzling off-leash recall, my most appealing credential for teaching this class, but needed work on heeling and needed to work with other dogs in close proximity. She is a very social dog, like Benson, and, in fact, acted as if class were a wonderful party that I arranged for her pleasure every Saturday morning. Gradually she came to understand that occasionally play breaks would be interrupted by work.

Our play breaks were a most important part of dog class. Even indoors, I do not run a rigid class. With less pressure, owners and dogs seem to have more fun while learning. Moreover, it is desirable in dog training to integrate the obedience work into the life of the dog as soon as that is possible. You do not want a dog who will work like a movie star in the local school gym and be a hooligan everywhere else. That happens all too often in traditional classes. As our dogs learned and took play breaks, we were able to *use* the commands in "real life" that the dogs were learning in class. We were able to call the dogs to come, sometimes as a group (best for reluctant beginners), and finally, one at a time from a romping group back to each owner. In addition, the dogs really enjoyed the release word OK because it not only meant a release from, let's say, the sit stay, it might also mean a chance to run and play with friends. Because we gave more—we let the dogs have fun—we got more—the dogs worked better. Play became much more than a way to let dogs blow off steam and then return to work. Play became a way to practice training. It became a way for us to observe the dogs and learn more about them. It became, for them and us, a reward for hard work. Watching the dogs move with grace and joy and humor was part of what got us all up on Saturday mornings. As time passed, we were all sharing a growing community, as it turned out, of dogs and humans. Communication deepened from owner to dog, among the dogs, among the people. Yet there were more happy surprises to come.

During most play breaks, Jamie would go off by himself and play with sticks. He adapted very well to training and was doing admirable work, but he did not choose to play with his fellow students. One day, as the weather began to get colder, and as we sadly began to realize that our class would be a dog class for *most* seasons and would have to take a winter beak, Jamie began to change. During play breaks, he began to play with and enjoy the other dogs. Sometimes he'd find an enormous stick and offer it for tug-of-war. Other times he'd join in on a group race or just hang in closer than he had before. We were all bursting with joy, but none more than Scott.

We all worked hard, practicing daily during the week, and the dogs progressed through the basic commands: sit, stay, stand, come, down, heel. Down was done cautiously because we were in the park and because three of the four dogs were male and might not care for this submissive posture. I demonstrated a most gentle technique for lying the dog down and asked owners to practice it at home rather than out in the park. The following week most of the dogs would lie down with little or no assistance, except, predictably, Jamie. He was, however, doing it at home and began to lie down in the park by the end of our session. Once the basics were taught, we began some advanced work. Since the class was small and the owners avid workers, we moved at a rapid clip. We began the fast or emergency down and the down from a distance, both excellent for safety. Mostly, though, we worked on the recall. Most helpful was working on individual, off-leash recalls where all the dogs are lined up on a sit stay and called in to their owners one at a time. Any dog who breaks when another is called is put back on a stay until his own name is called. This exercise reenforces good attention and really fast recalls when the dog is called. In addition, we worked with hand signals, sometimes working silently for ten or fifteen minutes at a time. We left the park and worked on Broadway, teaching the dogs to heel in crowds and not to leave the sidewalk without permission. The group looked wonderful marching down the block at heel. We all felt very accomplished.

Class time, which normally runs an hour for indoor groups, because of our setting, our human-dog community and our

Dogs entertain themselves during this class break for tactical conference.

strong enjoyment at the work and the play lasted for two to two and a half hours. Even then, we usually went home because we were freezing or starving, but not because of boredom. Despite this odd system of letting students come and go, of mixing young and old dogs, of working outdoors, of working off leash with beginner dogs, of meager economic return, I judged dog class in the park to be highly successful and planned to begin again immediately after the thaw. With a little help from my friends, I had identified a need in my own community and had filled it in a sensible fashion. For an incurable dog lover such as myself, the rewards of such work are rich indeed.

A DOG CLASS IN YOUR NEIGHBORHOOD?

If the idea of effective, reasonable, local training appeals to you, here is what you can do about it. First, check the resources in your own neighborhood. You will need space, preferably where dogs gather and play already, and you will need a trainer. You can contact the local kennel club to see if they can recommend someone with training ability who might like to do a class. You can even volunteer to help spread the good word and assist in class. By using flyers instead of the local newspaper, you can keep costs at a minimum. There should be some charge for class, though. People tend not to value what they get for nothing—and the trainer, whether an experienced professional or an enthusiastic amateur—should not be asked to work without pay.

Local training classes can do more than civilize a neighborhood's pet dogs. In the case of neighborhood classes, dogs and owners learn in a community setting where fun and friendship, both human and canine, are an integral part of the package. An outdoor class, a dog class for most seasons, can prove that a big city can be a wonderful place to raise and train a dog.

TAKING YOUR DOG TO SCHOOL

It's very possible that classes are already being held where you live, either through the local kennel club, in a school gym, at the community college or under the auspices of a professional trainer. In that case, go and observe. Before you sign up, make sure you like what you see—because what you see is what your dog will get.

Here are some criteria to consider:

1. *Number of dogs in class.* Divide the number of dogs by the number of instructors and then by sixty. That's how many minutes of attention you and your dog can expect. If you have one teacher and twenty-five dogs, you can see that class will be too big for you unless you are very confident or have a very easy dog.

2. *Instructor's attitude.* Some trainers run class by making fun of the owners to shame them into practicing. Others treat even the shyest Sheltie as if he were a fulsome, chunky Rottweiler. That's no way to run a dog class. Even though it is easier for the instructor to be soft and sweet in a one-on-one situation—partly because he can be heard without raising his voice—still, it is possible to run a dog class and be polite and respectful to both human and dog students. No, folks, this doesn't mean I'm a wimp! Class, as all things, must have balance, being neither too soft nor too hard, neither too serious nor too silly. Dogs can and do get trained in an atmosphere of friendliness. Why shouldn't they, when you think about it?

3. *Counseling.* Can you ask questions about behavior problems? Some instructors are "believers," others are not. Find out if you can get help when you need it.

4. *Fun.* Fun in dog school? Well! What a notion!

WHAT WILL YOUR DOG LEARN IN SCHOOL THAT HE WON'T LEARN FROM THIS BOOK?

Of course, now that you are reading *Mother Knows Best*, you will be able to teach your dog all the basic commands and then some. You can season him by working him in busy areas, near children, near other playing dogs. But in class he will get a chance to work *with* other dogs. This will add much to his presence, his self-assurance and to your confidence in him and in yourself as his handler. He will learn how to listen more carefully, not only coming when called, but not coming when not called. His ability to pay attention will increase. His consciousness will be raised.

Class is fun and social, too. Your dog will enjoy working with other working dogs. He may compete or show off, the little ham. You'll enjoy the other owners and the chance to brag about Buddy's high IQ.

Class will make you practice. You'll want to do well, maybe even best. It's humiliating to show up each week and have the worst dog. So, you will work Buddy if you take him to school. And that's good.

In class, you'll get to see all the commands, corrections, affections done by an experienced professional. That can be very helpful. You'll see good and bad handling in the students. You'll begin to see the difference and be able to monitor your own training better. You'll see you're not the only one who has trouble with the down or the come. You'll laugh a lot. Your dog will get trained. You may even get a diploma when you graduate.

Dog school, however, will not replace practice. It is, in fact, based on your hard work at home between each session. But if you are not working hard because you need someone to "give you the eye," class might be just the thing to get you practicing. One way or another, you're going to have to get Buddy trained for all those sweet, important fringe benefits. Class might be just the way to do it.

HOW TO GET THE MOST OUT OF CLASS

Some people show up at class every week and still end up with an untrained dog. In fact, some people (not you!) even brag about having an obedience school dropout. Somehow they figure if the dog does well in school, he's a ninny, a spineless wimp, an unnatural character, a poor reflection on them. A *real* dog wouldn't be caught dead being obedient. Perhaps they identify a bit too strongly with the dog, thinking of themselves as free spirits, mavericks, untethered souls.

But the dog cannot live well like this. Ask his mother. He's a pack animal. He craves rules and regulations, limits, work to do, a feeling of usefulness and participation, a strong, benevolent leader, an authentic dog's life. Sadly, lots of free spirits end up as traffic casualties or biters. Does this mean the trained dog is a robot who forgot how to be silly? Of course not. Every word in this book is aimed at helping you to educate your dog so his safety will be assured and he can have a full, rich, fun life. Being untrained won't make a dog a free spirit any more than not taking baths will make you an untethered soul. There is something there already in your dog, maybe it's the call of the wild, that you cannot own. There is a "dogness" there you can only begin to admire, but, try as you will, you cannot possess it or even fully understand it. Trained or not, he'll always be his own dog to a degree. He is yours to enjoy and care for. You can neither change his true nature nor keep him forever. So don't use silly excuses for not training your dog.

You can get the most out of class by wanting a trained dog. Then, practice, practice, practice—just like your mother used to tell you. Next, become an amateur naturalist, observing and learning from the other dog/owner duos. You may see some things you'd like to change (wishy, washy praising; corrections that do nothing; excessive harshness). You'll want to be right on target, the way mom would if she were here. You'll take mental notes. You'll get there.

Perhaps your dog will be light years ahead of the other dogs. Maybe the instructor will let you do drop-line work while the other dogs work on leash. The same class, after all, can be used in many ways. The bully can do a sit stay in the middle of the other working dogs. The shy dog can get applause for his work. Class can be a gem with many facets.

GAMES TO PLAY IN DOG CLASS

One of the nicest ways to make sure that class doesn't turn out a bunch of robots is to play games right in class. The games can be aimed at instructing owners, tightening training for the dogs, illuminating behavioral truths, having fun. They also make time fly.

211

Musical Dogs

Here is a game ideal for class because even beginners can play. After a few weeks of basic training, dogs are put on sit stay while owners proceed to the next dog in the circle. Each owner will work each dog in class in turn until the game is over. Each dog is then, of course, being worked by each owner. Indoors, the procession can be made with leashes dropped. Outdoors you can hold the leash until it is taken from your hand by the owner behind you, and so on. The initial exchange is great for the dogs. Some may try to take off when the leash is dropped. Good. Let them and correct them. Now each dog must learn to pocket his anxiety and jealousy as he watches his owner work each other dog in turn. In addition, he gets better and worse handling than yours. The better trainers will give him some superior practice time, teaching him respect for good control. The weaker handlers will confuse him for the moment. He may begin to work badly. But then the game proceeds and he'll be whipped back into shape. There's a good lesson here: Don't be too quick to judge. A good correction is always around the corner! The game is a real eye opener—and fun—for owners and dogs.

Monkey in the Middle

Each dog gets to sit in the middle of the circle of working dogs. When the dog is rotten—your basic neighborhood bully, a biter, barker, a rotten creep—rename the game Monster in the Middle. But even the sweetest beast will learn doubletime by having to contain himself while all else is moving about him. The monkey's owner should stay outside the circle, even if it means the trainer must keep her foot planted on the monkey's leash. No dog having been monkey for five minutes will ever give you a hard time on the sit stay again.

The Out of Sight Recall

This game or exercise will escalate the level of training in class remarkably in one session. With the dogs lined up on sit stays, the owners depart. One at a time, from an out of sight, hidden area, they call the dogs. If a dog leaves and tries to find his owner when he is not called, he is corrected. If he does not go when he is called, he is corrected and made to go to the spot from which his owner called him.

Monster in the middle.

The out of sight recall.

213

The first few rounds of this exercise are wild to see. Usually when the first dog is called, all the dogs break and dash out madly to find their owners. By the third trial, the dogs begin to get it right and it's beautiful to watch their self-assurance, control, alertness, pride. This is a great group exercise that does wonders for the recall and for mutual confidence between owner and dog.

Come, Don't Come

I admit that this is not a game. It's an exercise. But why get technical. Dogs are lined up on one mat. Then they are called one at a time. They are called on signal from the instructor and in random, changing order. Each time, the dog called must come and none of the dogs not called must come. This exercise teaches dogs to listen carefully for their master's voice and their own name. No daydreaming in this game. It is just as important that the dogs not come when another dog is called that they do come when they are called. As you might imagine, that will take some time to iron out and you'll have a lot of work and fun doing so.

Recess

A confident teacher who knows her dogs can give the class recess, the way we did in Riverside Park. In our case, the dogs were all playing off leash in the park every day anyway. So each owner already knew what was involved in getting his dog back. Of course, we also knew that none of our dogs would bite or run away.

As we continued to work on the recall in class, we got the chance, too, to practice calling the dogs back from breaks. Thus, we integrated training into the lives of the dogs and the owners, making training smoother, more reliable, useful, real.

Once your dog will leave a play group to come when called, he's on his way to becoming a superbly trained dog. Recess, then, is more than a rest. Rather than being an absence of training, it is the finest use of training you'll ever see.

Class can help make training fun for you and your dog. It's social. It's entertaining. It's educational. It's not only a great place for dogs. Class can also be a great place to raise and train humans.

9

Off-Leash Dog

If one word does not succeed, ten thousand
are of no avail.

Chinese proverb

YOUR DOG'S SENSE of pride will be one of your greatest assets in doing advanced, off-leash work. Given the heady opportunity to work in freedom, untethered and responsible, your dog will develop a kind of scorn for the leash. Sure, he'll still get excited when you take it off the doorknob for his walk. But when he can manage without it, you'll see a different animal. You'll see natural pride. Will you still think of him as a dumb animal, incapable of understanding the implications of his education? Not a chance.

It will be your dog's pride, in fact, that will now become a chief tool of training because when your dog delivers the kind of graceful, accurate, attentive work necessary in an off-leash dog, he will get to work without a leash more often, for longer periods of time and in increasingly interesting surroundings. When he goofs, tests, errs or daydreams, his leash will be snapped back on with a dramatic flourish and he will continue to wear it *for the rest of that session.*

As your dog gets hooked on the feeling of freedom that he experiences working off leash, he will concentrate better and try harder to obtain that feeling again and again. Praise and corrections, then, will come largely from himself. Just as we absorb the important early lessons our parents teach us, so he will absorb a kind of mental set about off-leash work. Does this mean, once this is accomplished, we can be inattentive while walking on busy streets with our dog heeling free at our sides? No. It does not. The dog, no matter how educated, is still imperfect. Some *thing*, who knows what, is always capable of drawing his full attention and allowing him to forget for a potentially fatal moment that he is on command and responsible to you. (Full attention equals dog chasing squirrel.) So when you are too preoccupied, too tired, too entranced to pay attention to your off-leash dog, keep him on leash. His pride in his work will be a great and visible tool to aid you in his education. But he will always be a real dog, a distractible dog, not a computer. If you cannot determine to give your dog your full (think SQUIRREL) attention each and every time you remove the leash outdoors, stop his training at this point. If you've *really* come this far, you already have a dog whose training will dazzle not only the average but the above-average dog owner. Your dog does not have to work off leash!

If, on the other hand, nothing but *the works* will satisfy you, hold on tight because we are about to take off.

DOWN FROM A DISTANCE

Getting your dog to lie down when he is not near you will take some work on your part, but it is not as difficult as it looks. It is, in fact, a very flashy looking command and will impress anyone who sees your dog do it. That aside, it is also the prerequisite for a good emergency down and it is therefore an important part of insuring your dog's safety when he is off leash. If you see danger coming and can keep your dog safe with a word, it will be less risky to work him off leash. In our book, it's always safety first.

With Buddy on a sit stay and you standing in front of him, signal DOWN in the usual way, bending and patting the floor in front of him as you issue the command. Praise him and tell him to sit. If he does not sit, slip your hand into the collar and pull straight up, repeating SIT as you do. Now tell him to stay and back up one giant step. This puts you one giant step from a correction. Raising your arm straight up *as* you say the

216

Raise your arm straight up *as* you say DOWN.

command, say DOWN. This is the distance or field signal, used because it can be seen from very far away. If Buddy responds with a down, lower your arm, praise mildly and tell him STAY. After a moment, release him, praise very warmly and try again.

If your dog does not respond to the familiar word and unfamiliar hand signal, step one step forward with your arm reaching for his collar as you step. Slip the hand that gave the signal right into his collar, pulling down as you repeat DOWN. Now, praise him, even though you made him do it. That's how he learns. Now move him to another spot and try again.

While your dog may seem terribly unclever when he fails to lie down when you say DOWN and raise your arm instead of patting the floor, he has a right to be confused by a new signal. He is not dumb. It just might take him a few turns around the block to get used to the distance signal. By the end of your first session on the distance down, he should be lying down with you signalling from six feet away. Always be prepared, especially in the early stages of training, to rush back to him and correct him with the hand that gave the signal in one sweeping gesture. Thus, the correction is implied in the hand signal, reminding the dog that even though you are far away, you can still correct him quickly. No matter how well things go, though, do not increase your distance for a full week after reaching six feet away. If you go too far too fast, your dog will get the notion that you no longer have good control over him. In fact, if it takes you much longer to get to him, he will become convinced that his suspicions are correct. So, as usual, slower is faster, particularly when working at a distance.

Once the dog has mastered the down from a distance at a distance of six feet, you can do two things. Gradually increase the distance, working farther away when he is cooperative and alert and shortening up the distance when he seems to be having a bad day. In addition, once he will readily drop from a distance, begin the next stage of your safety work, the emergency down.

THE EMERGENCY DOWN

The emergency down is one of several insurance policies that will enable you to take the risk of some day taking your dog off leash in the street. This is taught after your dog will do a very good down but it is executed differently. First, it is taught in an emergency tone of voice and because of this it is practiced no more than twice a week. If you practice this too often, it loses its punch. You might then end up like the boy who cried wolf, not getting the help you cry for exactly when you need it most.

In order to teach your dog the emergency down, first think MOTHER. Like Buddy's mother, you will teach via use of body language and tone of voice. If you use these elements properly, you will quickly and efficiently communicate to your dog a sense of emergency and a need on his part to comply with your command *without hesitation*. And that is the point of the emergency down. Once learned, it can be used to stop your dog in his tracks—to stop him from dashing out into traffic, from leaving your sight, from entering a danger zone that you understand and he does not. In fact, the very point of instant obedience is that you can foresee dangers that he cannot comprehend. The dog must not, therefore, take the time to look around and figure out whether or not he should obey you. He must obey without thinking. Like Rick in Casablanca, you will do the thinking for both of you.

When teaching the emergency down, as you are heeling along, lean forward, slide your hand into the dog's collar and *as* you push your hand straight to the ground, say DOOOWN in a serious, hushed tone—as if something were terribly wrong. Don't use an angry tone. After all, your dog hasn't done anything wrong. Use a tone that lets him know there's trouble brewing and he'd better drop fast. As soon as he does, even with your help, praise him and tell him to heel. This is not a down stay. It is an immediate drop that we are after.

Practice three of these within half a block of walking and then do not use this command again for three or four days. Keep the element of surprise in it by using it sparingly. Remember, this is taught so that, if you need it, you can use it to save the dog from an accident. You don't want to be like the boy who cried wolf.

What if your dog is a slow worker and takes his sweet old time to lie down, deliberately moving one leg into position at a time? You may decide to let him do his other commands at that

Slide your hand *into* the dog's collar—

push to the ground, saying DOWN—

praise and say HEEL.

pace, but not this one. If he's not quick in an emergency, the command, and your insurance, are worthless.

Continue to speed up the down by placing your hand *inside* the collar (not in the ring) and pushing it straight down to the ground as you say DOOOWN in a secretive tone. Once the dog knows this command and will execute it rapidly, practice only once in a while. At that time, make sure that some of your practice is done when he is off leash in the yard or in the park. After all, in order for this command to be an insurance policy, it must work and work superbly when your dog is off leash and not particularly near you.

In the park, you will have to be louder to be heard. But even so, what if nothing happens? Rush to your dog, grab his collar, repeat the command, push your hand straight to the ground as you do. With your dog's leash back on him, heel your dog and repeat the emergency down two or three more times. If you still feel *very* patient and full of energy, let him loose again and after five full minutes, try the emergency down at a distance once more. If he ignores you, repeat the above procedure, but after the practice, simply take him home.

Now when you get ready to work with him again, work on the down from a distance and not the emergency down. Obviously, he is not ready for such advanced work yet. When his down from a distance is *terrific*, go back to the emergency down and try it again. You may be thinking, "What's the difference?" One is done with a hand signal (and sometimes voice, too) when the dog is far away from you but looking at you. The other is done whether or not the dog is attentive—usually, not. Either might work in an emergency. For my dog, I want every bit of insurance I can get. How about you?

Drop on Recall

Many dogs will do the drop on recall better the first time you try it than ever again in their lives. This is because the element of surprise is so powerful that first time that the *trained* dog simply complies with the command on the spot. Later on, wise to what will follow the drop, he tends to come more slowly and drop quite slowly. For this reason, this command is used sparingly. If not, you will really slow up (translated: mess up) your dog's recall. Yes, You!

But, used carefully, this command can be a life saver. If you call your dog and then see danger approaching the path he is taking, you can stop him by dropping him and save his life in the process. So, do not use this flashy command again and again to prove yourself, your dog or to entertain your friends. Teach it and then save it for an emergency. A word to the wise is sufficient, no?

Once your dog will readily drop from a distance on verbal or hand signal alone, you can begin the drop on recall. In this command, the dog is afar. He is asked to come and then dropped (given the down at a distance command) when he is half way to you. In practice, the dog can be dropped at almost any time along the way so that if you need to drop him at any point, you will be able to do so. In order to teach your dog to do this, place him on a sit stay at some distance. Six feet will not do since that would allow him to get too close after the COME before you had a chance to drop him. Ten or twelve feet should do the trick. Call Buddy to come. When he is one-third of the way toward you, raise your arm in the distance signal and say DOWN in a good, strong, firm voice. Your dog may drop on the spot. If so, wait one hippopotamus and then call him to come, using both voice and hand signal for come (a sweeping gesture is used, arm moves from out at your side to your chest, as it would if you were calling a human chum from a distance). When your dog gets to you and sits front, love him up like crazy. Try one more and move on to another command.

If your dog does not drop when told, run to meet him and drop him with the raised hand that gave him the down signal. This procedure works very well and, with patience on your part, all dogs can learn to accomplish this very stunning looking but practical exercise. Practice twice a week, no more than three times each session.

What if your dog does an excellent drop on recall but consistently creeps in on the come, expecting every plain recall to turn into a drop on recall? In this case, and it is very common indeed, work on exercises to speed the recall and defer practicing the drop for a couple of weeks while you do so. Call the dog

223

THE DROP ON RECALL

225

to come and run away from him, turning at the last moment to let him catch you. Praise wildly. Occasionally when you are heeling the dog, break away without warning and call COME, COME, COME to him. Again, let him finally catch you and be praised. Play recall games with several family members calling the dog to come in random order and zestfully praising him when he does so. Then, too, when you do practice the drop on recall again, only do it once or twice, following it up with some fast, active work, some speedy straight recalls and lots of praise.

Don't Even Think About It!

Many years ago, when my Golden Retriever, Oliver, became a reliable, off-leash dog, I began to use the colorful phrase, "Don't even think about it," to prevent problems. If Ollie and I were out for a stroll and I spotted a dog across the street, I'd wait for the moment he first spotted the dog (you can tell exactly when that is by watching for an increased alertness in the dog's ears), then I would say, "Don't even think about it!" and smugly watch his ears return to their normal, nonalert position. Moreover, he would even look elsewhere, not wanting to see the temptation that he couldn't have.

Of course, Ollie and I amused a lot of people with our "Don't even think about it," and that was fun. But more important, the phrase, properly timed and properly intoned, worked! This fine piece of insurance can save you having to use the emergency down, the drop on recall, the shout, the hysterical fifty-yard dash. It's even good at home. It can prevent the loss of a choice roast or fine piece of brie, too. But in order to use it effectively, you need what I call *dog eyes*. That is, you have to be able to look at the world as your dog would see it, spotting the temptations that could spell trouble *just before he does*. Then and only then does the colorful warning work. If you try it after he has left your side to chase the squirrel or after his lips are surrounding the brie, it will be as useless as jerking the leash your loose dog is not wearing.

You may edit the sentence to suit your own personality. What you say is not the issue. The important points are owner alertness, timing and tone. Once established, a warning sentence can be used when the elevator door opens (even before

226

Don't even think about it!

you see if there's another dog waiting to get on), when your dog eyes the roast, when your off-leash dog sees a squirrel hightailing it across his path. Again, as established alpha dog in your pet's eyes, your warning tone is something he must pay attention to. Therefore, whatever he was planning is scrapped when your warning comes. As you can see once again, perfect timing is essential in off-leash work.

No! Come! Wait!

You have already taught your dog the commands NO, COME and WAIT. Yet these three strong words will be three of your best tools in off-leash work. Of course, if the dog does not respond to them, they are of no use. And if your dog's response to them is spotty (no pun intended), they might be worse than useless. In that case, you might have the illusion that you could control your dog by shouting NO. Then, sadly, you might find out that the day you really needed your dog to listen was the day he played deaf. So before taking the leash off your dog in an unprotected area, one of the things you must do is tighten the three little words that you will come to count on for his safety.

You may have noticed that I used the word *shout* above. I chose it carefully. The only time you should shout at your dog is when that might be the only way to get his attention or stop him in his tracks when there is danger. If, on the other hand, you scream and shout at your dog day in and day out, he has already learned not to listen to you. He already tunes you out as effectively as you tuned out all your harsh, abrasive, big-mouthed teachers when you were a little kid in school. If you are a screamer, stop now. In fact, for several weeks, stop talking to your dog altogether. Work him silently as much as possible. (Note to a certain person—you know who you are: whispering isn't allowed!) When you simply *must* speak, *then whisper*. Get your dog's attention back. Make him look at you to see what you want. Learn to yell at someone your own size instead of your poor dog. This will make your dog attentive and ecstatic.

Now that you see it will work, always speak softly to your dog. Now if one day you should see your dog heading lickety split for danger, you can shout to save him. By all means, if Buddy is headed for the railroad tracks, shout NO, WAIT,

To speed up Buddy's recall, run backwards as you call him.

Come, come, come. Goood dog!

229

The short line or tab.

COME! In this case, do anything you can to save him and get him back. In the meantime, save your heavy ammunition and don't shoot it off every chance you get.

The Drop Line and the Short Line

Now you can begin the work of teaching your dog to be as reliable off leash as he is when he's wearing one. It will go slowly. Nothing flashy will happen. You'll have to be patient. You may even want to quit in the middle. You can, of course. But if you do, don't think you didn't. Do not take your dog off leash in an unprotected area unless you and he can truly handle that responsibility successfully.

You will need two tools for this stage of training: a drop line and a short line or leash tab. A drop line is a long leash—10, 12, 15 or 20 feet long. The cotton canvas ones are cheap and easy to work with. You will work the dog in a protected area just as you did when he was a puppy, first lying the leash across your palm and then dropping it to the ground as you heel along. Since the drop line is so much longer than the regular leash, it may take your dog some time to get used to it dragging behind him. He may walk bowlegged or sideways at first. Let him work it out. He will. As you train, alternate between the drop line, the regular leash and the short line or tab. This is a piece of equipment you may have to make yourself. Many of my clients used leather key chains made to be worn on belts and merely eliminated the ring. Others made small leashes from old leashes or broken ones, cutting them down to a comfortable size. The tab is a little leash, just big enough for your hand to grasp. It dangles from the collar. Its weight is a small reminder to the dog of your control and presence in his life, even when he is "off leash." It is one of the best training tools ever and, at this point, your dog should wear his most of the time. The short line or tab allows you to make a professional feeling correction even though your dog is not *on leash*. The feel of the tab hanging from his collar can remind a dog that even though he is *free,* you can make corrections. So even when he is far away, the tab will remind him to come when called. ALPHA it says. MOM it says.

For now, we want to confuse your well-trained dog a little.

The tab makes a professional feeling correction even though your dog is not "on leash."

By alternating leashes and by sometimes using *more than one at a time*, we will confound the dog. He will cease to know when he's on leash and when he's off. In addition, he will be unable to know which kind of a correction you can deliver and from what distance. He may just give up and behave!

Sometimes you will hang the tab on the dog's collar and add his long line. Then after a warm-up, you will remove the long line with a flourish and continue working. The dog will not remember if the tab is on his collar or if he's totally free. If he errs and you can make a good correction with the tab, he'll *know* you are all powerful, alpha to the max! Even an assertive dog can be dazzled by the two-leash method.

Staying in a protected area for at least the first month of training, continue to work on all previous commands and all new safety commands with the regular leash, the drop line, the tab, alternating in no particular pattern. Also, as you work, test your safety devices off leash with the fence bolted. Try the drop on recall, the emergency down, the serious come, no, wait. But, still, do not work them to death or make them into a game.

Now you can begin to work your dog in the park. Use both the short and long lines so that when you take the drop line off, the dog is still wearing *something*. After he is working well on drop line, take that off and remind him immediately to heel. If he lags or moves out to the side, make a sharp correction with the tab and then praise him. Work only for a few minutes so that at the time you quit he is still working well. Do not push him into errors. Instead, build the time he will stay with you and obey you smartly without his leash and in this exciting, new environment.

When you are really confident, when Buddy is sharp and obedient on all the safety commands, begin to try stays and comes from a distance in the park, first with the long line dragging and then with just the tab. If he is attentive and obedient now, you may begin to work him on the street.

When you first work your dog on the street with a drop line, work when the street in your area is least crowded and when traffic is lightest. First, there's the problem of distractions, which you do not need at this most difficult stage of

Now you can begin to practice in the park.

Good dog!

training. Second, there's the mechanical problem of people stepping on your dropped long line, unintentionally giving your good dog a correction. In order to concentrate fully—and so that your dog can do the same—keep your first street lesson very short and work when no one is around. Of course, your drop line is dragging so that if your dog tries to run off, he will not be harmed. You will simply step hard onto the leash. Then, too, you have checked and rechecked all your safety commands and, even if you must say so yourself, your dog's work is excellent. Otherwise, why on earth would you be trying to do off-leash work in an unprotected area—right?

Plan at least a month for each new stage of training to make sure your dog behaves reliably even on his bad days. So after a month of work in the park and a month of drop-line work on the street, you should be ready, if that is what you choose to do, to try working on the street with only the tab.

By now you are an expert on your dog and his behavior. He is well trained, better than most dogs you have ever seen. You have tightened all his on-leash work and have worked on all his off-leash work for months—indoors, in a fenced area, in the park, with the drop line, with the tab and on the street with the drop line. So now, after a run or a hike and after some good obedience work in the park, take your dog to a familiar, quiet street and heel him, holding onto the leash tab. Now, drop the tab and heel him for half a block. Before you get near the corner, stop, have him sit, praise him. While you're at it, praise you. Now, pick up the tab and heel him home. Each session, build his confidence and your own, until you have the dog you want.

If you have longed all your life for your own version of Lassie or Rin Tin Tin, you are well on your way. You may never want to work your dog on busy city streets off leash—in some places, that is punishable by stiff fines—but certainly by now when you run your dog in the park, you are sure he will come back when you call him. Moreover, if you have long pictured yourself strolling contemplatively down a country lane with your dog at your side, that image can be a reality. And, if, like me, you really do love the idea of taking that quiet stroll with your off-leash dog on a busy city street, because that is where

Correct with the tab when you must.

Pretty soon your dog will correct himself with just a tap on your leg.

you happen to live, you are well on your way toward that goal, too. You have to keep working with the tab on your dog's collar and your full (think SQUIRREL) attention on your dog. Pretty soon, this kind of practice—and pleasure—will become second nature to both of you. So while you are making this new life style with your dog, here are some final points to keep in mind about off-leash dog training.

1. Your dog does not have to be off leash every minute of an off-leash walk. If you meet a friend, see a great store window or find some other tempting distraction, snap the leash on your dog until you can once more give him your full (think SQUIRREL) attention. I use the leash to cross Riverside Drive because the potential for danger (five lanes of traffic) is too great to risk my precious dog. Sure, she's good. But this is the route to the park—to other dogs, to running free, to squirrels. Besides, what do I (or you) have to prove?

2. Always keep a leash with you, even when you plan to keep it off the dog—just in case.

3. Whether or not you think the dog needs it (he does), reenforce your alpha position daily. The best nonviolent way to do this is with the long down (one-half hour will do). This is problem prevention at its finest, and easiest.

4. Don't ever expect great concentration from your dog when he is all pent up and needing exercise. Always give him a good run before off-leash street work.

5. Be sure you don't get lost on one aspect of dog ownership— training, showing, control. Remember that your dog has a wide range of needs. In fact, remember that you do, too. There are times when it's great to get wrapped up in yourself and leave your dog at home.

6. Even as your dog gets older, give him reminders of your alpha-ness and reviews of his training. If he doesn't use it, he'll lose it. Is that true for you, too?

7. Keep the love and high spirits in your relationship with your dog. When seeking fine control, don't forget to play some games and have some laughs. Dogs love to crack jokes. If you don't know that, look again when you play with your dog.

238

The long down is problem prevention at its finest.

8. When training and behavior look messy, don't be afraid to go back to square one and tighten everything up again—on leash. No one's watching!
9. Don't forget the larger goals: good communication, mutual admiration and understanding, good times, respect.
10. And don't forget—mom. When you have doubts about the course your relationship with your dog has taken, when you have questions and you just aren't sure of the answers, think again about your puppy's mother, her style, her natural, intelligent, effective, humane way of getting things done. The more we know, the more we think we know, the more Mother has yet to teach us.

And don't forget mom—her style, her natural, intelligent, effective, humane way of getting things done.

10

Games to Play
with Your Dog

Give and take makes good friends.

Scottish proverb

PLAY IS AS IMPORTANT for you as it is for your dog. People, too, are animals and play is an important and special tool of all animals, young and old. It is through play that young animals test out a whole variety of adult roles and skills. While you might have played house, fireman, lion tamer or nurse, puppies play at chasing and catching, tugging and mock fighting. Play continues into adulthood in both species, still serving as a safe arena for practicing skills and trying out roles.

When your dog was just a tiny puppy, he learned many important things from his mother and with his littermates. Much of this learning was accomplished through play. Give small puppies a string and they will reinvent the tug-of-war. Give them a little space and they will hide and stalk and pounce, practicing for a life in the wild they will never know. They will climb and crawl, run and freeze, use their brand new voices, find things by scent, wag their tails and play and play until they can do nothing but fall down in a heap and sleep.

Play can be active, helping muscles grow strong. Play can require intelligence and cunning, helping minds grow sharp.

Much learning is accomplished through play.

Play can require intelligence, cunning, daring.

Play calls for daring, originality and humor. It is a wonderful and delightful way to exercise and strengthen everything you've got—mind, body and spirit. This, too, is true for your dog. In addition, by playing with a creature of another species, you will profit from his special skills and language as he will from yours. In play as in training, you will experience the fascination of cross-species communication, a new and exciting way to share affection, time and fun with your pet.

MIRROR GAMES

Mirror games are exercises in concentration and mutual mimicry. Since the action in both these games is small and specific, play them after your dog has had a run and is a little tired. That will make him more willing to do something intense and quiet.

To prepare your dog to play mirror games, sit on the floor with him so that you can look at his face and he can, if he chooses to, look at yours, just as if you were each looking into the mirror. Your dog may be reluctant to look straight at you because for dogs a direct stare is an aggressive act, a show of dominance. However, your dog will learn, as most pet dogs do, that all the customs of the wild don't necessarily hold true in human households. He will not have to hunt for his food nor live in a cave. And a stare between man and dog is not necessarily an expression of dominance. It may be, on the contrary, an expression of love and kinship. If your dog will not look you in the eye, make some kind of little noise to get his attention—a click, a low whistle, a hum. Any noise he likes will do. If you then praise him when he looks at you, even if it's just a quick peek, he'll begin to feel more comfortable about looking at you because you are telling him that it's okay. He'll also be more apt to do it again and again. Praise makes him feel terrific and any time he feels terrific, he'll want to repeat whatever it was he just did. So as you play and as you praise him, he'll be more willing to look at you for longer periods of time and with better and better concentration. That will make him a more attentive playmate and a better gamesman.

Dogs are very prone to copying and mimicry. But even in

Play requires concentration—

and mimicry.

the best of circumstances, every dog won't copy every action. Your dog might never brush his teeth, give himself a bath or learn how to make lasagna. But he can and will copy a lot of interesting and humorous facial gestures and body actions. Body language, as you know, is his chief form of communication. That makes him a highly observant fellow, quite adept at playing mirror games.

COPYCATS

Your dog is already an expert on you. He learned to watch you carefully long before you thought of playing copying games with him. He depends on you for his food, his walks, for a warm, snug place to sleep, for fun and for affection. So his eye is on you whenever possible. He *needs* to read your moods accurately so that he can stay on your good side, so that he can anticipate a wonderful walk or know when the time is right for a snack or some affection. He knows the meaning of all your body language, moods and gestures.

You can think like a dog. Watch your dog carefully, quietly and without interfering or interacting. See how he holds his ears when he feels loving, angry, scared, excited, playful. Note the variety of tail positions. Check out the way he uses his paws, his head, his body. Watch him play with other dogs and see if he's a nose bumper, a jumper, a racer, a circler. Does he "box" with his paws, lean on his pals, play lying down? Once you discover his own particular, individual gestures, you can copy each and see if you can add to the universal dog gestures described below.

There is no correct order to these games, no rules, no penalties, no points, no losers. Any time you play copycats with your dog, you'll both be winners. Whenever you experience the secrets of communication with another species, for that single moment you will have made a wonderful connection. Your dog will know it. You'll know it. That's all that counts when you play copycats.

Panting: The less subtle the action, at first, the easier it will be to make your dog notice it. For that reason, when your dog is still a novice player, begin with an action that makes a sound, such as panting. All dogs pant. If your dog is shy about looking you straight in the eye, the *sound* of you panting will get his attention. He may begin panting without ever looking at you. No matter. The game is officially on as soon as one of you imitates the other's action or responds with a comparable action. That is, your dog may respond with an exact imitation. In this case, panting will evoke panting. He may also respond with another sound or gesture that has the same meaning. Since all the sounds and gestures in these games indicate a friendly, playful mood, *they are all interchangeable by either of you.* If you pant to your dog and he paws the air in your direction or he sneezes or play bows, he is reading you clearly and answering you in kind.

Dogs pant when they are hot. That's how they sweat and cool their bodies. Dogs also pant when they are happy and feeling friendly and sociable. Thus, panting to your dog is a most eloquent and propitious way to begin any game. Before you begin, get comfortable with your dog by sitting on the floor next to him. That alone will make him begin to feel very special since you are joining him on *his* turf. Now, sitting very close to him, either face to face or side by side, begin to pant. He may get very excited. He may appear to be startled. After all, this may be the first time you attempted to speak *his* language, a language he was born to understand. At this point, your dog should respond in one of two ways. He may, after an initial display of surprise, begin to pant along with you. Notice how the gesture resembles a smile on both of you. Or, he may, being adept at this language, translate your gesture before he responds. In the latter case, he will test your ability in a foreign tongue by reacting with another gesture that also indicates his friendliness and willingness to play. Next, your dog will begin to watch you and to concentrate on you. He has gotten your message and wants to know what's coming next. So keep things interesting for him by keeping them moving. A good game has both action and surprises in it.

Play Bow: Did you ever see your dog bow to another dog? This gesture, which resembles a stretch, is part of the body language of all canines. It is the method dogs use to invite play. It is aptly named the play bow. If you bow to your dog, he will understand the invitation. He will bow back and be ready to begin a game. You can bow and get a bow back in return as part of playing copycats, or you can bow to invite your dog to play any game you and he enjoy. This is not a gesture to repeat and repeat such as the sneeze. Once invited to play, your dog will accept and be ready to go on to the game of your choosing or his.

Lie Down: In order to bow properly to your dog, your knees will be on the floor, your body bent forward, your "paws" on the ground in front of you. Since you're half way there already, you might as well lie down. You're probably not playing in your tux anyway. Chances are strong that your dog will lie down next to you. Chances are strong that if he's got a tail, it's wagging. But if he does not respond by imitating you, don't force him to—even if he is trained to lie down on command. Part of the deal of game playing is that it is voluntary. He can ignore a "round." He can quit in the middle and walk away. His freedom to do or not do is what makes the game most wonderful when he does!

Roll Over: Now you can play out the old joke of the human trying to train a dog by doing all the commands himself. For training, there *are* better methods. For games of mimicry, doing the thing yourself is what the game is all about. Or, at least, half of what it is all about. As long as you are lying down, why not roll over? This will probably send you from your side or belly to your back. Your dog will probably continue to copy you. If he hesitates, rubbing his belly will help him make up his mind.

Pawing: At any time during these games, your dog may offer you his paw. Even if you taught him to give his paw as a trick, he is pawing now because it is a submissive, affection soliciting, friendly gesture. All dogs, trained or not, paw to ingratiate themselves to their owners and to receive affection. You can answer by imitating him with your "paw" or by grasping his paw with yours and giving his a shake. If you haven't done it so far and it pleases you, you can name the gesture while you're at it.

Sneezing: Dogs sneeze to clear their noses for fresh new scents. Better still, they sneeze when they are happy. Your big or small sneezes might work all by themselves to get your dog to sneeze. If not, you can do a little detective work. Observe your dog to discover just what makes him happy enough to sneeze. He might sneeze when *you* wake up in the morning or when *you* get home from work. He might sneeze when he sees his bowl, his bone, his leash or a roast beef. Wait for the right moment. Now he's the leader. He'll sneeze. You sneeze. He'll sneeze. You sneeze. If you're a big ham, you can add some drama to your game by using a big handkerchief. Keep sneezing. When your dog sneezes in response, praise him and sneeze again. See how long you can keep the action—and the communication—going. If your dog sneezes when he's happy, will he be happy when he's sneezing? Anything's possible!

GAMESMANSHIP

Keep in touch with your dog as you play—by eye contact, by word, by touch. Encourage him to keep copying you or responding to you by praising him for doing so, by scratching his head, back or belly, by talking to him in a tone he enjoys, by copying him and by panting. Go back and forth between human language and gesture and dog language and gesture so that you each become "fluent" in the other's tongue. Experiment as you play to see what gestures in particular are part of your own dog's vocabulary and to find out which things he enjoys most. The more you play, the more he'll like these games and the faster and better his responses will be. Remember, too, that he is capable of initiating a game, so be on the look out for him to make a gesture with the intent that you copy it.

Each time you play copycats with your dog, you increase his ability to play this game and any other game. Playing makes him smarter, stronger, better able to concentrate and observe.

When thinking play, always think MOTHER. Mother knows best. She knows that this is one place where puppy can win. She lets him feel his oats and play at being king. She knows she can always remind him of her alpha-ness with just a sound if he gets too big for his britches. (For you, that sound is ENOUGH.) She lets him stretch, but she keeps a balance. She's beautiful to watch, cavorting with her puppies. Here are some more active games where you can be beautiful playing with your dog, just like mom.

248

CATCH ME? CATCH YOU!

Now that I've got a herding dog, I have become an expert at losing races. So can you. This brings up another important point in gamesmanship. When you want to invent some new games of your own to play with your dog, go back to the breed standard. There you will see the skills and abilities bred into your dog, generation after generation. You can translate these skills into game work. (If you have a mixed breed dog, maybe you can work backwards, noting his talents and then guessing at the breeds that composed your most special combination dog.)

By contemplating the serious work a dog was bred to do, you will even be able to predict how much he'll like a given game and even how, exactly, he'll play. For example, do you imagine that a herding dog would let a sheep outrun him? Get the picture?

Many dogs love racing games, but for herding dogs, these games are bread and butter. You can play indoors with your little puppy or outdoors with your off-leash trained dog. In fact, if you run for the phone at home, your herding puppy probably already beats you to it. In the hall or in the yard, you can tear through space feeling exhilarated at your own speed, grace and agility. But in your heart, you know your dog, Old English Sheepdog, Sheltie, Shepherd or mutt, is about to cut you off at the pass. So be it. Remember mom. This is *the* place to let your dog win, as opposed to letting him win in a test of wills or when you issue an obedience command.

Indoors or out, you can establish bases. Scarlet and I work from the bed in the back of the house, through two halls (we both skid a bit on the hairpin turns), through the living room and to the old, beat-up couch near the front door. The round ends when the last of us (guess who?) to jump onto the base gets pounced on by the winner (guess who?). The new round starts with a lot of lively faking—and then one of us makes a mad dash for the other base. Interestingly, the dog does as much faking as the owner, which is one of the reasons why I love this game so much.

Of course, you can add any rules you like to the game. You can add additional dogs or people. The variations are endless.

However, if the excitement of the game gets your dog to escalate his general vigor and good humor into biting, simply correct him. (Think MOM.) Do not give up the game. After all, this is one activity your kids will want to participate in, too. So, continue this wholesome, constructive exercise, using your ENOUGH command if your excited dog begins to mouth you or nip.

THE PROTECTION RACKET

Barking games are among my favorites because they have so many benefits and spin-offs. But first, find out what makes your dog bark. Is it a knock on the door, a biscuit held out of reach, the sight of another dog, a car in the driveway, or, if you have a terrier type, dust settling? Be ready to say SPEAK, SPEAK, GOOD DOG when the stimulus is there to trigger the barking. In no time, you will have a dog who barks on command. Reward him when he does so with a resounding GOOOOD DOG.

You might also get your dog to start barking by barking with him. So what if people think you're crazy. What do they know? If your dog likes to bark, he might like to howl. Tilt your head back and give it a try. Group howling is natural for dogs and they love it.

Now you can switch your dog to a hand signal for barking. For example, point your finger at him and say SPEAK, GOOD DOG, SPEAK. As he catches on, alternate voice plus hand signal with hand signal alone. Within a week, your dog will bark when you point at him. Now you are ready to have some fun. Ask your dog to add two and two and point at him. When he finishes the fourth bark, say GOOD DOG and pet him. Now ask him for the square root of twenty-five. Now ask him to bark your age. Now call Johnny Carson. Once your dog barks on a hand signal, you can really go places.

My Golden Retriever, Oliver, had a yearly stint at a young friend's birthday party. He'd show up fashionably late, just in time for the cutting of the cake, and bark the young lad's age. Then all the kids got to watch Oliver eat birthday cake, which he did in even less time than it took him to bark *five*. Oliver liked the performing end of game playing and you and your dog might enjoy it, too.

The ultimate racket your dog can make, though, is the protection racket. When Raffles comes to call on you, call on your barking dog. Signal him silently to bark and say, "Get him. Good dog. Who's there? Watch him!" Fun with sound can lead to sound protection.

ROUGHHOUSING WITHOUT TEARS

It wouldn't be right to leave the area of game playing without a word on roughhousing, that which can help you really enjoy your puppy, that which, if handled badly, could get you into a lot of trouble.

Roughhousing can be pure fun. It can blot out the stress of the day. It can get the heart and lungs working at their peak. It can make the worst grouch laugh and laugh—even this one.

All dogs and most owners love to roughhouse. If you monitor—and *only* if you monitor—this is a great way to play with your puppy. Watch any litter at play. Roughhousing is a natural expression in young animals. You will see hiding and pouncing, shoving and pushing, winning and losing. And, you will even see monitoring. When a puppy gets hurt, he will signal with a cry. He may even withdraw, and that is respected. Thus, puppies learn how to play without harming one another. And they learn, through rough play, the pecking order of the litter.

When you rough it up with your puppy or dog, you must monitor, too, and you must keep in mind that your puppy is learning the pecking order of his new family. So if you let him hurt you, if you let him be too rough, he will imagine himself top dog of your pack. That, needless to say, is a large *no-no*.

When you roughhouse with your dog, you are teaching, too. You must be able to regain control in an instant, even in a mock fight. The word to use is ENOUGH. Like his mother, you will be a reminder of reality when things get out of hand.

Let's go back to nature once again. Observe the way the mother plays with her puppies. She lies down and lets the puppies do most of the pouncing. When a puppy gets too rough, she stops him, gently, with her paw. The puppy gets the message, pronto. By the same token, the mother does not

252

provoke the puppy into a frenzy, as some misguided dog owners do with their pups. She may tease, but she'll only tease to get the puppy to follow her or pounce on her. She will never work him up so that he attacks or grabs on or bites, tugs and shakes. She keeps a wonderful balance, even in her play.

If you enjoy roughhousing, add it to your dog games, but limit the time you give to rough play and limit the roughness as well. Be sure that what you are doing is appropriate to the size and age of your dog. Be sure, too, that you are not accidentally teaching your little dog something you will not want him to do later on—when he's bigger or when you're not in the mood. Try to play as another dog would—or as his mother would—never hurting the dog or frightening him, never causing him to defend himself or get frantic, never allowing him to have a permanent upper hand or to call the shots. Also, make sure you can end the game when you want to. Most important, make sure that nothing the dog does hurts you. That, indeed, is the bottom line. If play hurts, it's no good. And that's true for both teams.

Play can keep the balance in a humane-canine relationship. It keeps you aware that dogs are not only furry little things that make stains on rugs. They are, also, creatures with zest, wit, originality. If you are open and willing to learn while you play, if you allow your dog to change the rules, to change roles with you in play, to expand upon the games, you will find him to be more fascinating than you ever dreamed. Play, perhaps, will help move humans from our minimal understanding of dogs toward a richer, deeper, more realistic knowledge of our most charming fellow earthlings.

Keeping appropriate precautions in mind, thinking *active* rather than *rough*, when it comes to dogs and people, play's the thing. It is a natural expression for each species, a perfect arena for friendship, education, humor, joy and love. Play is the ultimate reason for having a dog, the best reason for mimicking mother, the very sweetest part of Mother Nature's glorious and perfect design.

Way back then, in those thrilling days of yesteryear and right on down to our own time, working, playing, struggling and surviving, hard times and easy, it's been man and dog. So be it. You can't fight history!

There is something in your dog that you cannot own—maybe it's the call of the wild. There is a dogness there you can only begin to admire, but, try as you will, you cannot possess or even fully understand it. Trained or not, he'll always be his own dog to a degree. He is yours to enjoy and care for. You can neither change his true nature nor keep him forever.

INDEX